Spooky Creepy
New England
2

SPOOKY CREEPY
NEW ENGLAND 2

Karen Mossey

Schiffer Publishing Ltd

4880 Lower Valley Road • Atglen, PA 19310

Designed by Danielle D. Farmer
Type set in BeooSans R11, R12, R13/Book Antiqua
ISBN: 978-0-7643-4502-9
Printed in The United States

Schiffer Books are available at special discounts for bulk purchases for sales
promotions or premiums. Special editions, including personalized covers, corporate
imprints, and excerpts can be created in large quantities for special needs. For more
information contact the publisher:

Published by Schiffer Publishing, Ltd.
4880 Lower Valley Road
Atglen, PA 19310
Phone: (610) 593-1777; Fax: (610) 593-2002
E-mail: Info@schifferbooks.com.

For the largest selection of fine reference books on this and related subjects, please visit our
website at **www.schifferbooks.com.**

We are always looking for people to write books on new and related subjects. If you have
an idea for a book, please contact us at
proposals@schifferbooks.com.

This book may be purchased from the publisher.
Please try your bookstore first.
You may write for a free catalog.

Dedication

I dedicate this book to my children and especially to my grandchildren, who are true believers in the paranormal. Young minds are open to the phenomenal and uninhibited by the influences of the world. They are more likely to tell you their experiences in total truth. The more we listen and encourage them to tell us, without criticism, about their actual experiences, the more we can learn from them. I love you guys and may we have many more ghostly adventures together.

I would also like to say a special thank you to my spiritual "Sister" and mentor, Elizabeth. As my true friend of fourteen years, she has guided and encouraged me along the way through many trying times and laughed with me during the good times. She has shown me the positive in all things. Her unwavering support and faith in me has been my crutch through the years. Our bond is eternal and I truly believe we have been in many lives together. I love you, "Sista."

Acknowledgments

I thank a few of my many special friends who played a major role in helping me with some of the stories within this book. As always, I could not have completed this book without my good friend and partner in the paranormal, Mike Sullivan. He is, without a doubt, my top confidant in paranormal research. We have known one another for over forty years, during which Mike has provided me much indispensable information.

In addition, I extend sincere appreciation to Carrie and JW Cox. We have had so many great paranormal investigations together, and a lot of great times as friends. I met them several years ago at an investigation and we have been good friends ever since. (www.awakennhspirits.com)

My friends from Hudson Cable Television (HDTV), Catherine and her husband Harry, and our good friend Karl, have followed and filmed us on many paranormal adventures and made us a part of their series, *Spectral Evidence*. I look forward to joining them each month to talk about all things supernatural.

No investigation is complete without Leo and Linda Monfet. Leo's infrared photography is unsurpassed.

My gratitude goes to the best psychic medium I have ever met, phenomenal April Sheerin. She has inspired me and mentored me for over twelve years, on "Spiritual Thinking."

I am sincerely thankful for the opportunity to have joined Tom Spitalere and his team and all of those who attended this really amazing adventure. I am also grateful to all of those who supported me and purchased my book *Spooky Creepy New England*.

I thank the team at Schiffer Publishing, who enable me to share with you my "Spooky and Creepy" adventures in this book.

Contents

Preface

When thinking about the contents of this new volume of *Spooky Creepy New England*, I wanted to add in a personal mix of not only paranormal encounters during investigations, but also stories of my own and those of others' personal experiences with supernatural occurrences, synchronicity, and signs from those who have already crossed over. There have been many communications received by the living from those in the spirit world. These unexplained, phenomenal signs and stories, by what can only be attributed to spiritual intervention, along with evidence gathered during paranormal investigations, further validate the continuance of life in some form other then a physical body. This is what we refer to as the Afterlife. I believe our energy and consciousness continue on and remains intact even after the physical body dies. It is this interaction with the spirit realm that we seek out through our research into the paranormal. It furthers our understanding of what happens to us when we pass on and why some spirits choose to remain close to the physical plane as ghosts. They usually will interact with us in gentle influences and not the scary way that is often portrayed. The more we open up to and work with them, the more sensitive we become to this other existence. We will, after all, be part of this very same Afterlife someday. The more knowledge we have about it now, the better will be our understanding of what awaits us after this life is over. We can find peace and joy and live a quality life, where and when we can, without an overwhelming fear of death.

Karen Mossey
Paranormal Investigator, EVP Specialist

Mike Sullivan
Paranormal Investigator, EVP Specialist & Reflective Photography

Leo & Linda Monfet
Paranormal Investigators, Infrared Photography & Videography

April Sheerin
Psychic Medium

Rocky Morrison
Paranormal Investigator

Massachusetts

1.

Hilldale Cemetery
Haverhill, Massachusetts

Two graves in the paupers' section of
Hilldale Cemetery. *Photo courtesy of Mike
Sullivan*

Two children's graves in Hilldale Cemetery.
Photo courtesy of Mike Sullivan

Well, I never thought I would be having a book signing in
a cemetery at eight o'clock at night, nor did I think I would be
delivering a presentation on EVP (Electronic Voice Phenomena,
which are messages resembling disembodied voices that are
inaudible to the human ear at the time they are recorded, but heard
upon the recorder on playback) where the podium I was speaking

from was the top of a headstone. (I made sure to say a quiet *thank you* to the individual laid to rest there.)

This remarkable opportunity and adventure was extended to me by Thomas Spitalere and his paranormal team Essex County Ghost Project. Tom is also the curator of Hilldale Cemetery and the best expert to be found on the historical aspects of the site. Not only is he a very adept paranormal investigator, but he is also an excellent tour guide who knows every inch of this cemetery and its history. He was great at intertwining a macabre mystique with the actual history and paranormal encounters that he and his team had bore witness to over the many, many visits he has had here. The entire night was rich with the story telling of ghostly encounters, legends, and lore from Tom's expeditions into the confines of Hilldale Cemetery.

The night was absolutely perfect for a cemetery walk and investigation. It was warm and dry. The stars adorned the sky and, though it was dark, the evening was clear enough to see the gravestones and twisted and knotted trees. It made for a very eerie sight. This was just what we wanted.

The evening started out with a very flattering introduction by Tom to bring me on. He is like a radio and television host personality and after he was done promoting me, I wondered if I could live up to everything he had said. Tom had brought a complete PA sound system which proved to be so helpful when I began playing the EVP. I placed my equipment on top of the headstone, stood a little to the side of it and began addressing the crowd of eager paranormal enthusiasts that had come out for this amazing event. I started off with a quick explanation of what EVP was and asked for a raise of hands on how many of the folks were already familiar with it. Almost every hand went up. It is remarkable how this aspect of paranormal evidence has become so well known and essential to the field of paranormal investigations since it came to the forefront for everyday people as well through the movie *White Noise,* starring Michael Keaton. At this point in the presentation, I thought it would be appropriate to play one of my EVP that was used in the trailer of this movie and played my father, Stanley Searles, exact voice in recorded a year after his passing saying: "I love you."

As the presentation continued, I played several of my clearest EVP to really get the adrenaline hyped up for this evening's cemetery investigation. With each EVP, I could hear the excitement and anticipation of the crowd with their "*oooohhhs* and *aaawwhhs* and *wows*." It really made me feel good but, of course, it is our Spirit communicators who really are responsible for these incredible messages. I finished up with one of my most interesting and also the longest EVP I have ever recorded. Appropriately for the location we were in, this EVP was from Hills Farms Cemetery and is a minute and forty-four seconds of non-stop voices, pops, thuds, and clicks with the sound of swirling wind-like noise throughout the entire clip as if a portal or vortex had opened and then suddenly closed directly over my recorder. (This EVP and the story that surrounds it can be obtained on our website at www.ectoweb.com in Our Paranormal Evidence section under Hills Cemetery, the first listing.)

Following the presentation, I did a book signing from a table we had set up in the cemetery.

The Investigation Begins

We then proceeded into the cemetery for the investigation. Tom separated the group into three parties; two being led by two of his team investigators and the other was being directed by Tom himself. I was asked to accompany Tom's group.

Fright Night

Our first stop was near the entrance and off to the right in a section of the cemetery where Tom told us the tragic story of a man who, three years prior, was found dead in his car on the exact stop where we were standing. He was apparently the victim of a drug overdose. We decided to do an EVP recording here. I asked if there were any spirits present with us at this moment and in this place and, upon playback, I heard a very clear EVP in the voice of a woman say "YES!" Everyone in our group took a gasp when they also heard this very clearly. This was a great piece of evidence to start off with and lead into this ghostly investigation. Now everyone was really pumped up for a paranormal "Fright Night."

From there, we proceeded to the "Paupers Area" of Hilldale Cemetery. It is a sad sight to see so many unmarked mounds where the towns unfortunate are interred. Some of these graves are just marked with a wooden cross or small statues and plastic flowers. Some, more than likely, are not even placed six feet down, as mounds above the level of the ground were clearly seen.

A Two-pronged Message

I felt chills throughout this area and some of the investigators were sure they had seen dark shadows moving about and then disappearing behind the trees. Tom decided this would be another good place to do an EVP session. I turned on my recorder and Tom began to invite the spirits to give us a message. All of a sudden, something pulled on the back of the hood on my jacket so hard I was jerked back and I said, "Hold on," and shut off my recorder. I quickly spun around only to find no one behind me.

I was not afraid, but rather excited that what had just happened was not caused by someone in the group, but would have to be attributed to something out of the ordinary. Whenever something phenomenal like this happens, it always gives me such a rush of excitement. It is a startling surprise because it comes so quickly and unexpectedly that fear does not have a chance to register until after the encounter, and then it usually does not happen again.

What makes this so much more interesting is to get a validation of this physical attack through the EVP message I received at the moment it happened on my digital recorder, just before I shut it off and turned around. Upon playback, I heard an EVP message stating very emphatically, "I'm gonna strangle you!" Was this mean-spirited ghost trying to strangle me by tugging on my hood? I find it so amazing how what I could not see could cause a physical influence over me.

A Lost Leg

We then proceeded to "Hangman's Hill," where Tom had felt there had been an Indian battle. We formed a circle and drew upon the energy of the area by holding our hands together. Tom is a psychic medium as well as a paranormal investigator and told us he was going to begin to channel in the ghosts. He told us not to break the circle because this could cause him great pain while channeling. In one exciting moment here he asked for anyone present to show us they were there by making something move or stop moving. There was a large flag pole in the center of the circle and the American flag that was blowing in the breeze suddenly fell quiet and remained perfectly still for the remainder of Tom's contact.

He then revealed a Civil War soldier had entered his body, telling us that he had lost his leg in a battle and was looking for it when he died and could not rest in peace. He gave his name as Charles Morris and the name of his wife, Abby. Then Tom fell silent ...and he dropped to the ground. The soldier was gone and he once again became conscious of himself as Tom. Several members and participants experienced bouts of nausea during the event. The level of activity and paranormal phenomena was high this night. Sometimes, if you are not fully grounded in the physical dimension, exposure to different vibrations and energy from parallel dimensions can make you uneasy and you may feel sick.

Seek and Hide

Our last stop of the evening's investigation was on to an area where Tom felt he could connect with the spirit of an Indian Guide and the ghost of a little girl. Having a deep-rooted connection to the cemetery, he had sensed the spirit of this little girl many times. He told us she likes to play "hide and seek" or as she referred to it "seek and hide" with him whenever he is in the cemetery.

We proceeded to the top of the hill where Tom told us there had been a battle between soldiers and Indians. Strangely, while moving to the top of the hill, several members, myself included, smelled the strong sent of gunpowder. Spirits often manifest their presence through the sense of smell.

It was fast approaching 11 p.m. and we needed to gather everyone together to close out our very exciting investigation at Hilldale.

Hilldale Cemetery has all things creepy that you might like to experience...if you dare. But tread carefully, there may be someone there who wants to strangle you!

 ## Hilldale Cemetery
Haverhill, MA 01830

Visit the website www.eagletribune.com/haverhill/ x1750256439/City-receives-complaints-about-Hilldale-Cemetery to read about vandalism, illegal dumping, and maintenance problems being among concerns for this location.

2.

The Haunted Houghton Mansion
North Adams, MA

Vintage postcard: The Houghton Mansion.

Mike, Leo, and I, and our good friend, Psychic Medium April Sheerin, had the pleasure of being speakers at a recent conference hosted by Harvest Moon Paranormal at the very haunted Houghton Mansion in North Adams, Massachusetts.

The mansion has a long and emotional history deeply rooted in tragedy. It is said that there are several spirits that remain in the mansion. Three of those are tied to the Houghton family themselves and one is believed to be a little girl named Laura, who some say, has a connection to a previous building that stood where the mansion stands now. It is thought that the building was a church that was destroyed in a fire. Many believe Laura's death was connected to this tragedy. She is primarily felt in the basement of the mansion and has been known to move toys and balls that people have placed there for her.

The most famous ghosts of the mansion are those related to the Houghton family. It is believed they remain trapped there because of a fatal car accident that lead to the demise of four individuals: Mary Houghton, Sybil Hutton, and eventually, John Widders and Albert Houghton.

Mr. Albert Houghton held the prestigious honor of being the first mayor of the town of North Adams, Massachusetts. One beautiful August day in 1914, the family took their car, a Pierce Arrow, out for a drive to Vermont. Mayor Houghton's servant and family chauffeur, John Widders, was driving. While attempting to avoid a crew of workers in the road, John steered the car around them and lost control, sending the car tumbling down the side of the mountain.

Sybil Hutton was thrown from the car and then crushed when the car landed on top of her. Mary Houghton was critically injured and succumbed shortly after from her injuries.

Devastated and guilt ridden over what had happened, John Widders committed suicide the following morning and died from a self-inflicted gunshot wound. He was found near the barn.

Unable to cope with the loss of his devoted daughter Mary, Albert Houghton died nine days later, his health failing.

In 1920, an addition was built onto the Mansion and the Houghton Mansion then housed the Masonic Temple that is sustained by the Masons and the Eastern Star. The Masons have done a beautiful job of preserving the mansion and events, such as the conference, contribute to the well being of this beautiful, historic, and very haunted building. Mary's room, Mr. Houghton's room, and the room of John Widders seem to be the most conducive to paranormal activity.

The Investigation Begins

The conference culminated with an investigation at the Mansion. People packed up their paranormal equipment and set off on an adventure to explore the building in hopes of experiencing something paranormal. In one room, a small group circled a table and questions were addressed to any ghostly presences that might be there. It was amazing to see the K2 meters (a specific kind of electromagnetic meter) around the table lighting up in perfect synchronicity in response to the questions. In Mary's room, a group sat quietly as conference director Kim Huertas channeled information from the spirits. It was very interesting to later confirm, through one of the masons, that almost all of the information she gave was accurate.

Mirror, Mirror

In the servants quarters upstairs, where John Widders room had been, we discovered a closet housing a psychomanteum. A psychomanteum is a chair set before a mirror in a darkened room with just the light of a candle behind the chair. The mirror is placed slightly above the chair so you cannot see your own reflection, but rather you gaze up into the mirror as if scrying to see if spirit images or scenes from otherworldly existences will appear. I decided to lock myself in the closet, in the dark, to see if I could capture any EVP messages or experience any images that might appear with the dim lighting within the mirror. After a short time, I began to feel somewhat nauseous and left. A second person also entered the chamber with the psychomanteum and came out feeling the same way. The energy was just too dense and depressing there.

EVPs

I captured several interesting EVP during the investigation of the mansion. In one EVP, as I was entering the kitchen area, I asked, "Is anyone in here?" I received a reply saying my name: "Karen." It always makes me wonder how can they know this. Are they the resident spirits or my guides or loved ones that often go along with me into haunted places for protection?

In a recording captured in the main room on the first floor, originally a dining area, I asked if Mr. Houghton minded that we were in his home and a ghostly voice answers in an EVP saying: "Noooooo...I'm happy you're here."

One other interesting capture was recorded in the basement where the little child Laura is often felt. Though it is hard to understand exactly what is being said, it is clearly a woman's voice that was heard on the recorder on playback.

It is always exciting to visit the very haunted Houghton Mansion when you are in North Adams in the beautiful Berkshire Mountains; and you will probably get spooked by at least one of the resident ghosts that dwell within the mansion when you visit!

 The Houghton Mansion
172 Church Street • Adams, MA 01220

The Mansion is currently used as a Masonic lodge and houses Lafayette Graylock Lodge A.F. & A.M. and the Naomi Chapter of the Eastern Star.

To find our more about the history and hauntings, as well as special events, visit The Berkshire Paranormal group at their website http://berkshireparanormal.com.

3.

The Witch City
Salem, MA

"More Weight."

The Author takes a photo with a dark angel near the witches cemetery in Salem, Massachusetts. *Photo courtesy of Carrie and JW Cox*

The Author with the corpse bride in Salem, Massachusetts. *Photo courtesy of Carrie and JW Cox*

Salem, Massachusetts, is a remarkable place; but never as extremely exciting and bizarre as in the month of October, for the season of All Hallows Eve or Halloween. This is the witching season and Salem becomes a mecca for crowds of people that include just the casual observer, like me, and those who dress the part. If you can get past the hour-long fight for an expensive parking spot and the multitudes of people, you are in store for real live entertainment unique to this extreme city. Adults and children, the old and the young, really get into the spirit of Halloween in Salem. They wear costumes and makeup to become whatever their wildest imagination wants to create during this month of festivities. Candles in Dixie cups light up haunted tours on every corner; sometimes two and three excursions within the same space. There are curiosity shops filled with potions, crystal balls, and psychics for Tarot, palm, or spiritual divination readings. The Peabody Essex Museum is in the heart of the city and there are numerous wax museums displaying the chronological history of the Salem witch trials. Zombies, witches, and ghostly characters roam throughout the streets, so bring your camera and get a picture of you with your favorite monster. Then, at 8 p.m., the haunted houses open and you can pick and choose which one or how many you want to go through. You won't get bored in Salem during the month of October. There is so much to do!

You do, however, need to bring your patience along with you, as the wait in the lines to the events may be over an hour.

The selection of delicious specialty seasonal foods abounds in Salem as well. The warm smell of hot cider and apple crisp drifts through the city streets. Food courts and stands are around every corner and you can fill yourself with chowder bowls, chicken tenders, french fries, and much more. Follow these main courses with a huge piece of fried dough or ice cream. It's all there for you. No one need go hungry in Salem. Nor go thirsty. If you just want pizza and beer, there are many cafés and sandwich shops. If you want club-style entertainment and beer, there's Murphy's and brew houses. A diversity of restaurants of many nationalities are all part of Salem's fine selection of eateries. Sit near the wharf, look out over the water, and partake in some seafood.

Spooky Tourism

The story goes that Salem, at one time, was a struggling city. The financial problems were apparent and the city was on the verge of bankruptcy. The mayor at the time came up with a brilliant idea to rejuvenate this fabulous and historical place. He decided to call it the "Witch City" and use the history of the Salem witches to establish and introduce tourism to the city. What transpired was just that and much more. The city attracted many psychics, mediums, and those who practice the art of witchcraft — and the city became their haven and claim to fame.

Salem is now the best known place in the country for those who refer to themselves as Witches or Wiccans and their craft. Salem is Witches and Witches are Salem. The tourism is booming, the revenue is growing, and Salem is once again financially stable. Thank you, Mr. Mayor.

A Pressing Engagement

Salem is a beautiful city situated right on the water. It is a wonderful place to visit anytime of the year. The cemetery and the memorial tribute and garden to all of the witches who were tried and executed by hanging is worth visiting while in Salem. Only one victim, poor 81-year-old Giles Corey, was executed other than by hanging. Giles was forced to confess to witchcraft or risk being pressed to death when boulder after boulder was piled onto a board placed on top of him. He did not confess and just kept saying, "More weight!" This was such a sad and horrific way for this man to die.

People who come to visit often place flowers and trinkets upon these sacred memorials in remembrance of this unfortunate and very tragic time in history and the loss of many innocent lives. I was told from a reliable source that there are no physical bodies actually in the cemetery and that they had been moved as the city expanded, but the cemetery remains much as it always appeared with ancient headstones and the names of those who were interred there at one time. It is a historical tribute that adds greatly to the ambiance of the city.

So if you love the excitement and entertainment to be experienced in the world famous "Witch City," Salem, Massachusetts, leave early, spend the day, bring your camera, appetite, and love for fun to enjoy a true adventure in the spirit of Halloween.

When Halloween ends and ghosts and goblins go back into hiding for another year, Salem becomes much quieter, but it remains the capital of Witch Central all year long and is a great place to visit at anytime.

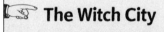 **The Witch City**

Salem Witch Museum
Washington Square
Salem, MA 01970
978-744-1692
www.salemwitchmuseum.com

Peabody Essex Museum
East India Square (161 Essex St)
Salem, MA
(Toll Free) 866-745-1876
www.pem.org

4.
Historic and Haunted
Franklin, MA

Named after Benjamin Franklin, historic Franklin, Massachusetts, is a small town we visited on a warm Saturday in June for an investigation of a private residence. This home had been built in approximately 1809 and had been moved to a different location three times before settling at its current marker. The current owners discovered broken pieces of tombstones in the backyard that had been brought in with a load of loam that had been dropped there.

The previous owner had done a bit of remodeling and closed off a staircase and entrance way that was used by servants that serviced this home and its owners in days long past. Theory has it, that when an old home that has had a long history of human occupancy is remodeled or changed, this can initiate paranormal activity, and the current owners can certainly attest to a lot of that.

Boys Will be Boys

One of the young children has seen a little boy walk by his bedroom door. This Spirit seemed to be particularly fond of and attached to the little boy who lives there now. He said he sees him all the time and describes what he sees as a moving shadow clearly resembling a little boy. He told us he is never afraid.

The family feels that the Spirits of a man and a boy haunt the location and that the man is the little boy's father. We later confirmed, through dowsing, that it was a father and his son who were there but, at the time of our investigation, the interaction came from the little boy. He was playful and had a very short attention span validated through evidence and signs of his presence being there for a moment and then gone the next. We believed him to be younger than 10 and his energy exhibited typical childlike behavior. At times, he caused the recorders to malfunction with his high-energy presence.

Some of the activity the owners have reported are the TV and TV games turning on and off by themselves. The family is constantly replacing light bulbs that burn out, even when they have just been changed. Footsteps are heard climbing the stairs and walking across the floor in the evening. The Spirit of the little boy is constantly poking the owners, especially the husband, and even pulls at his shirt tail. One might assume there is something particularly strange about the couch on the second floor. We took several pictures in a row and one would be dark and the next light, almost like a portal or vortex is present there.

Two Occurrences

The owners told us about two profound experiences they had. One evening, the husband was sitting in the living room (which had formerly been the dining room) and a blonde man with glasses walked through the main entrance of the house and into the living room and stood there looking at him. Then, within seconds, the blonde man vanished before the husband's eyes. He showed us the exact way it happened, saying:

> He came through the front door and stood here in the passageway to the opening of the living room. It is something I will never forget. I can describe him perfectly. He had blonde hair and spectacles and he was dressed like someone from a long time ago would have been dressed.

The other experience happened to the wife. She was sitting up in her bed in the bedroom (formerly the living room) leaning on her pillow, when the pillow rose up from behind her head, lifted her forward, and then went back down again.

Strange Evidence

We captured several strange pictures and EVP during the investigation, but we believe the activity was not very strong when we were there. We attribute this to the Spirits having sensed we were not part of the family. Apparently, they are very attached to and happy with this family and the family is, likewise, very happy with them being there. They made a point to ask us, "We hope that you will not make them go away. We like them being here." I informed them that Spirits leave only if it is their choice to do so. We are not allowed to interfere with their free will and can not make them leave.

Of the EVP we captured, one of the most interesting was one in which we clearly heard "57 people." Since we believed the home may have once been a meeting place, this EVP relating to many people would make a great deal of sense.

We thought we might be able to capture more evidence during a later evening investigation when the family might be away. They told us that most of the activity began after 9 p.m. So, perhaps, we will return for another round of evidence. This time at night with no one about, and see if our ethereal friends will stir some things up for us then.

5.

The Wreck of the
Jennie M. Carter
Salisbury, MA

Vintage postcard: The wreck of the
Jenny M. Carter.

2012: Wreckage of the *Jenny M. Carter* during extreme low tide; Salisbury Beach, Massachusetts.

You can still catch a glimpse of her at extreme low tide during a full moon. Her slowly decaying bones can be seen protruding slightly above the sand very near the shore. Over time her ocean grave has sunk deeper and deeper into the sands of Salisbury Beach, Massachusetts. Eventually, all physical traces of her will vanish. She will become only a memory, whose ill-fated voyage will be accounted for in the archives of historical records. Her legacy will live on in a few museum artifacts that are left to provide us with a testament to her demise.

Some say, amidst the roaring waves, the voices and wails and a dim shining light from a ship can be heard and seen on occasion, during the night of April 14th each year. Sadly, this tells us that the tragedy of the *Jennie M. Carter* may be a residual haunting of emotion and fear that replays year after year on that fateful night.

The *Jennie M. Carter* was a three-masted schooner carrying a heavy cargo of concrete slabs. She was twenty years old and met her end on April 14, 1894, near the site of the old Frolics, which was torn down in January of 2000. When rescue teams arrived, everything seemed in place and undisturbed, but there were no signs of any of the crew on board. An empty lifeboat later drifted onto the beach. None of her seven crew members survived. Only two bodies were recovered: the Captain, Wesley T. Ober, and Seaman Sven Siegfried Petersson, who was only 25 years old. The only survivor was a cat who was found on board the ship when she ran aground.

The last ones to see anyone alive on the *Jennie M. Carter* were the crew members of the schooner *Smuggler*, who observed the damage she had sustained and approached her. Captain Ober related that they had been hit by a spring northeaster. He insisted, however, that the *Jennie M.* was still solid and he could make it to land. Abiding with Captain Obers request, the *Smuggler* agreed and sailed away leaving *Jennie* to her fate.

What exactly happened after this is not fully known. Some historians believe that the crew tried to get into the lifeboat once they realized the ship began to come apart and a huge wave overtook them all, sending them to a watery grave. The only thing that is known for sure is that, other than the two bodies recovered, none of the crew was ever seen again.

Another Disaster

But the ocean around Salisbury Beach was not through claiming victims. A little over a year later, in February of 1896, the schooner *Florida* went to pieces off Salisbury Beach near the exact same dangerous area where the *Jennie M. Carter* met her demise. The similarities between these two disasters are uncanny. Both were three-masted schooners. Both had seven crewmen. Two bodies from the *Jennie M. Carter* and two bodies from the *Florida* were all that were recovered. Both attempted to launch lifeboats to escape. All perished.

Ocean storms and treacherous waters near Salisbury Beach, Massachusetts, and the surrounding areas have claimed many ships and their crews. Some say eerie lights and mournful cries of desperation are sometimes witnessed off the shores of the beach. Perhaps these lost souls are the ghosts of the sailors of the *Jennie M. Carter* and the *Florida* who long for one more chance to come ashore.

New Hampshire

6.

Spirits in the Chocolate Shop
Salem, NH

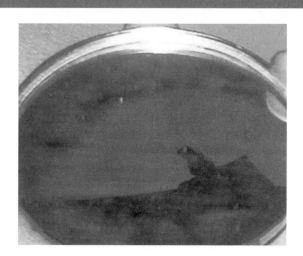

A photo from the chocolate shop using reflective photography in a mirror showing what appears to be a young girl sitting. *Photo courtesy of Mike Sullivan*

The team set out on a cold January night to investigate an older building in Salem, New Hampshire, which had been beautifully renovated into a candy and gift shop on the first floor, a wonderful café on the second floor, and a private apartment on the third floor — all of which were experiencing occasional paranormal phenomena.

The owner of the business had experienced shadows, sounds, and the feeling of being watched in both the shop and the café. The tenants had numerous sightings of a woman in an apron dressed as if in the early 1900s and a small child. They even had pictures that they shared with us, clearly showing a woman in an apron near their refrigerator and an image of the face of a little child. The activity was such that it was becoming disruptive. Their small son spoke of seeing a little girl who wanted to play with his toys. The parents complained of losing sleep because the sounds of pots and pans and cooking in their kitchen would be heard throughout the night. It became so bothersome, they thought of moving.

Every night they would latch the door leading to their apartment and lock it, and each morning they would find the door completely unlocked and open. They would see blue mist-like forms pass by them and shadows move between rooms. Their small son's toys would be found turned on when no one was in the room. Even while in the bathroom, they would feel as though some presence was in there with them.

Mike and I decided to leave several recorders in the bathroom to see if we could pick up EVP.

Setting the Record Straight

Psychic Medium April immediately picked up on the presence of several entities as she entered the building. One predominant spirit she sensed was that of a heavyset man who manifested both on the first and second floors of the building. She told us how he had come to the house during his lifetime when the home was a family residence, in the 1900s, and there was some unfinished business that he wanted to set straight.

He was seeking to proclaim his innocence from a matter that he had wrongfully been accused of involvement. April felt as though he had never remedied this and his tormented soul could not rest. She stressed to the owner and the tenants that neither this man nor any of the spirits in the building were negative, nor were they permanently trapped there. Some, such as this man, were simply seeking resolution, and others, like the lady in the apron, were just going about doing the things they loved and were so attached to during their own physical lives.

In times long past, one of a woman's main jobs was cooking in the kitchen. Little children would laugh and play with toys, like the small child spirit here would do. These types of paranormal activities are what we refer to as "residual imprints of past energy" that often play out, as they would have when these folks were actually physically here.

A Little Girl

April had also quickly picked up on the little child. She sensed that the Spirit was a little girl with pigtails that liked the little boy and wanted to play with the toys. We set up a ball as a prop, to see if it would move. We then left and went downstairs. But when we came back, we found it in the same position as when we'd left. Interestingly, the tenant's son was not home at the time. Perhaps the child had no desire to play with us, but chose to only interact with the tenant's son.

April told us that she felt that, at one time, the third floor had been the attic of the home and that the little girl had a bed there. A ladder led to the attic and, one day, the little child fell off the ladder and suffered an injury, to which she later succumbed. She said that this area was where the tenant's son's bedroom was now.

Sick and Dying

April went on to tell us how the house was originally a single-family home and the owners had several sons, some of whom went off to war. I asked her if any of the sons had died in the war, and she turned to me and said, "one did." This was later validated when the shop's owner produced a historical record from the original owners stating that they had four sons, one of which was killed in the war.

We asked the owner if she knew of any deaths that had occurred in the house during its long history. She did not know. She told us that, at one time, she knew there had been a room they referred to as a "sick room," which was located on the first floor. This led us to believe that there was a good possibility that a death may have occurred in the home. Even without an actual death having ever happened there, the strong energy and emotion of suffering and pain that would have been prevalent in a sick room might leave imprints of energy within a structure that can play out on occasion.

So that the family could once again gain peace and tranquility, and resume normalcy and uninterrupted sleep in their home, April and I asked the spirits visiting there to release their ties to the home and shop and leave the family to their peace. We told the tenants there was nothing to fear from these entities and they can ask them to leave if they chose. More often than not, this request does work. Many times, spirits are simply confused and need direction in order to move on. In one EVP recording, I requested that they release and move on. A soft questioning EVP response replied: "Release?"

It is our hope that this investigation may have helped put an end to the disruption the paranormal activity was causing to the family. We plan to follow-up with the owner and tenants to see if things are settled and once again peaceful in the building. April believed, with a little coaxing, the entities present would be able to move on. If necessary we will return for further evaluation and investigation.

Spirits can be anywhere and sometimes they just pass in and out. Sometimes events from the past, as in residual imprints, will play out now and then. It is important, though, for those of us now living out our physical existence to be able to be in control and live without disruption and fear. So, though we investigate to further our understanding and research in the paranormal, we always seek the presence of a psychic medium with us to help with drawing those in spirit near and perhaps assist with their transition beyond our physical dimension. This is always the best scenario, if and when it works.

7.
The Legend of Fody's Tavern
Nashua, NH

Fody's Tavern. *Photo Courtesy of Mike Sullivan*

Of all of the years I have lived in the Nashua, Hudson area, only rarely did I hear of the place originally known as The Tavern. It is now known as Fody's Tavern and has a charm reminiscent of days long gone. Upon entering through its wooden doors, it is like stepping back in time. One of the original fireplaces can be seen as you enter and the furnishings, complete with wears and tears illustrating much use and traffic through the building's long history, still remain. As you round the corner, you pass through a curtained doorway where you enter into a cozy bar and restaurant. Round little tables and comfortable chairs fill up one room and make for an intimate meeting and dining area. There is also a great bar and several round bar tables. They also have room for comedy shows, music, and live entertainment, which is a weekly occurrence at Fody's. The fireplace is always on and comfy couches and wooden tables make it almost rustic looking.

When my friend, Debby, and I visited Fody's, we felt so comfortable and took our place alongside many who appeared to be regulars. We really enjoyed ourselves and can see why so many people do become regular visitors. Sunday night's special is the biggest, juiciest burger you can imagine along with a mound of fries for a very reasonable price! You can't beat it! As a matter of fact, when you come in on Sunday the waiter asks you, " Would you like a menu or are you here for the burger?" Of course, everyone is there for the burger. Then compliment this great meal with one of my favorite ales, Dog Fish 60 minute IPA. They have all kinds of great food from the all-America burger to exquisite homemade desserts. Fody's is a must-visit Pub and so very historic. Old pictures and artifacts can be seen throughout the tavern. The doors open at 4:30 p.m.

Burgers Aside...

There is another side to this old brick, several-stories-high building. The tavern was built in 1831 and is rich in history, as well as its share of trauma and tragedy. This is part of the reason why The Tavern in Nashua must assuredly be haunted and the real reason that lured Debby and me there. With our passion for the paranormal, we were convinced we would experience something besides the great food and atmosphere. With the very first glimpse Debby had of the Tavern during her visit with us here in Nashua, she knew she had to go there. She even wanted to book a room and stay overnight, but the boarding rooms were in disrepair and being renovated at the time.

Even as a teenager growing up in the area, my dad always told me when we would drive up Main Street in Nashua, "Don't you ever go in there, Karrie, because that is not a nice place. Good girls don't go in there," he would always say. So being the typical curious teenager, I wanted to find out what made the Tavern so "taboo."

When I mentioned it to several of my friends, they told me that The Tavern was well known to be Nashua's house of ill repute or brothel and a haven for drug addicts and the city's undesirables. Up until into the '70s, it still had this reputation and rooms could still be rented out for such purposes. It was later closed down and then became the fabulous restaurant and pub that it is now.

Debby and I talked with members of the current staff when we were there and asked if they had ever experienced anything paranormal. We asked about the history to see if there was truth about what we had heard about the Tavern's past. We were told that it had a reputation for prostitution and drug addiction. The bartender told us the original building had been on the opposite side of Main Street and dragged across the street to where it sits now. It had been know as The Tavern, a place to get a cheap room, drink, and favors. The bartender believed there were two murders that happened there and she thought there had been numerous deaths. One story she had heard was that a mother, who was one of the "working girls," and her son were shot there. I couldn't find a record of this, but it would stand to reason that it could have happened. It would also seem probable that if it were a haven for drug addicts, there could have been many deaths from drug overdose. With all this being said, it was even more probable for Debby and me to believe that with all of the trauma, tragedy, and emotion over a hundred-plus years, there might be some paranormal things happening there. A great deal of residual energy must remain there within the walls and halls of the building and who knows what ghostly presences might still roam about.

Some EVP Time

We asked if we could do a few EVP recordings and take some pictures in the upstairs rooms. The staff was fine with us going up the stairs towards the rooms, but the rooms themselves were not open because they were unsafe during this renovation period. Debby and I were happy to have the opportunity to do this.

We asked the bartender if she would like to hear us playback any of the EVP captures we might pick up. She quickly said, " No." She told us that she had to close up at night and knows that the Tavern is haunted and that hearing EVPs would scare her even more. She had her own experience there one night as she was closing up. She was walking through the Tavern locking up and someone grabbed her shoulder so hard that it turned her around...but there was no one there. Ever since, she will not close up alone at night. I would say after something like that, I don't blame her a bit and find her to be one brave lady.

Debby and I sat on the landing at the top of the stairs leading to the locked door that would take us into the area of all the rooms. All of a sudden, we heard a door close from behind the locked door. Of course, there was no one in there...and it *could* have been the wind causing it...or, perhaps, they were telling us that room was being occupied by the resident unseen.

We asked several questions while our recorders were running, sure we would get a response from whatever spirits that were there—and it was likely there were several lurking about. It was no surprise that, upon playback, I captured a disembodied ghostly voice saying: "I think you can die here!" He was probably quite right and I am sure that several people most likely did meet their demise there.

It suddenly became icy cold at the top of the stairs. Theory has it that ghosts use the existing energy to manifest, drawing the heat out of the area and creating a bone-chilling cold. We also took several pictures as we left the landing and headed down the stairs. In one picture that Debby took we noticed a milky mist on one of the stairs. Could this have been someone following us down?

Our paranormal experience at Fody's Tavern, brief as it was, truly leaves us with a strong desire to re-investigate if we have the opportunity. It would be better to do this once the rooms have been renovated and reopened.

Meanwhile, for a great atmosphere, comedy nights, music, and entertainment, as well as very delicious food and drinks, take yourself and your friends on an adventure into the legends of the historical past—and be wary of souls from the past who might tell you that today is a good day to die here!

Fody's Tavern
9 Clinton Street
Nashua, NH 03064
www.fodystavern.com

8.
The 1875 Inn
Tilton, NH

The 1875 Inn. *Photo Courtesy of Mike Sullivan*

The 1875 Inn in Tilton, New Hampshire, is a beautifully preserved historical building, well over a hundred years old that has been visited by and accommodated many well-known people over its long history. Many of its rooms are even named after famous people, such as Thomas Edison, Henry Ford, and Mary Baker Eddy. It may well be that because they enjoyed the comforts of the Inn so much that a lot of residual energy and emotion remains behind from the days they passed through the doors of this great place.

For the purposes of our investigation, we were concentrating on the many souls that, according to several psychics, have checked into the Inn, but have not yet checked out. It has been said that as many as thirty ghosts haunt the Inn. We were hoping to make contact with the resident spirits, the most predominant of which, we were told, was a little 12-year-old girl named "Laura."

The infamous ghost of the 1875 Inn: Laura.
Photo courtesy of Leo Monfet

Apparition on the bed at The 1875 Inn. The author and Linda Monfet.
Photo courtesy of Leo Monfet

Fire

Laura's story is a tragic one. She lived in the Inn all of her life, and apparently still does. Her parents owned the business and often left bright and responsible young Laura to manage the Inn while they went out for a short period to tend to business. On one occasion, while Laura was minding the Inn, a fire broke out. Laura was trapped inside the Sanborn Room — this is the room I chose to stay in, although hardly the only room we experienced activity in. Tragically, Laura succumbed to the flames and perished in the fire before help could arrive to save her. She has been both seen and sensed in the Inn and is reported to love to play pranks and move things around. We had the privilege of actually meeting Laura through some of the amazing infrared photographs captured by Leo and several clear EVP examples gathered during our investigation there.

Signs of Spirit

The 1875 Inn was also the site of the Tilton jailhouse, which was located in the lower level of the Inn. We experienced some sudden cold spots while investigating in the area where the cells once were. In addition, we were told that there had been a suicide in one of the rooms in the Inn several years prior. The hostess told us that a man had taken his life in the room and was found by the woman cleaning the room the next day. She believes he is a troubled ghost that remains behind and haunts the Inn. On many occasions they have gone into the room where he died and have found the bed that had been perfectly made up in complete disarray. In one astounding photo that Leo captured, there is an apparition that appears to be lying down the length of the bed. At the same time the picture was taken, I also captured an EVP in a bone-chilling voice saying: "Laura!" So was it Laura resting there or perhaps the disgruntled ghost of the man who took his own life?

The chimney in the dining room, off where the Tavern area of the Inn is located, is original and still shows the blackened and charred side as evidence of the terrible, destructive and fatal fire that took the life of young Laura. Off this dining area is a breezeway leading to the entrance where Leo captured a series of incredible infrared shots showing moving spirit energy. The apparition took several different shapes as it moved across the area, as if trying to reach the door where, in the last shot, you can clearly see the image of what appears to be a young girl with her hair pulled back in an old-fashioned-style and wearing period clothing. We compared the image Leo captured with a picture of Laura in an album in this area and it appears to be match. The apparition in the mist in this picture seems to be a dead ringer (no pun intended) of Ms. Laura. We were happy that she decided to show herself for us during our investigation.

The 1875 Inn has been the sight of an archaeological dig, which discovered numerous historical artifacts. It has also been remodeled several times, which always seems to enhance ghostly activity. The resident ghosts don't always approve of changes and sometimes act up to show their protest. They seem to prefer things remain as they were when they were busy living out their physical lives.

I am sure you will be as thrilled with your visit to the Inn as we were and even, perhaps, be privileged enough to be granted the favor of an encounter with "Ms. Laura."

The 1875 Inn

3582 White Mountain Highway
North Conway, NH 03860
(800) 421-1785 or (603) 356-9025
info@the1785inn.com
www.1875Inn.com

At the time of this printing, the Inn was closed for renovations, which might stir up even more paranormal activity. For more information on the Inn and when it will reopen, visit their website or contact them for specifics.

9

The Halligan Tavern
Derry, NH

The Halligan Tavern. *Photo Courtesy of Mike Sullivan*

Inside The Halligan Tavern. Anomalies on window and
on the table. *Photo courtesy of Mike Sullivan*

Ready to Write a Book?

We're always seeking authors for a wide variety of topics. This is your opportunity to shine! See our website to view an extensive list of our titles. If this idea appeals to you, we'd love to hear from you. Review our book submission guidelines at our website by clicking on the "Submit a Book Proposal" link. Then email your proposal and ideas to **info@schifferbooks.com** or write to the attention of **Acquisitions** at the address below. You can also call 610-593-1777 to make an appointment to speak with an editor.

The Halligan Tavern was once the fire station for the town of Derry, New Hampshire. The original firehouse was built in 1883 and served the town for well over 100 years. The first full-time fire chief was a man named Frank Hurd. History tells us that in the early years of the Derry Fire Department, the fire engines were horse drawn and the water was carried by the firemen in buckets and placed in the tanks to fight the fires. It is interesting that during our investigation April said she could see back to the days before the firehouse was built, when the fireman were referred to as the "Bucket Brigade."

Additionally, before the building became The Halligan Tavern, it was a restaurant called the Fire Hall Pub and Grill. It seems that even when the first restaurant moved in, the paranormal activity began to be recognized and it continues now in its new venue, The Halligan Tavern. The wait staff has reported strange things happening, such as chairs and objects moving, lights turning on and off, and the water in the upstairs bar running when no one has been there. One waitress turned the water off, only to come back a short while later and find it on once again. They have heard footsteps on the second floor when no one was there and some of the staff have heard whispering in the upstairs bathroom with no one inside. April believes the spirits that reside there are not in full approval of the old firehouse as a restaurant.

The Investigation Begins

Several paranormal groups have investigated the pub and so we were honored to have the privilege of being invited to investigate it, as well and have our name added to that list of groups with the hope of capturing some substantiating evidence.

Legend has it that the first fire chief of the station, Frank Hurd, hung himself in the firehouse. Two theories as to why he may have done this are told. One is that he could not save two children who perished in a fire and this haunted him everyday. I could not find a historical record of two children dying in a fire during this time period, but

The séance at The Halligan Tavern.

I did find a record of two people who died in a residence fire in Derry in the 1960s. This, however, was way after Frank's time. The other reason he may have committed suicide, as the legend goes, is that he was so dedicated and devoted to his job that he worked incredibly long hours, which kept him from his family, the result of which caused too much stress on his wife and resulted in a broken marriage. I could find no record of Frank committing suicide, but our EVP evidence suggests that Frank's spirit is still diligently working and carrying out his duties as the fire chief at the station. Mike captured a clear EVP of a male voice stating his name as: "Frank!" But when we asked if Frank committed suicide, I also captured an EVP saying, "Nothing's proven." So the mystery of Frank's demise must still remain a legend.

April sensed a great deal of parties and special events that had been held in the firehouse. She saw visions of many men in uniform—not just the fireman but also soldiers going off to war. She saw happy times and much laughter there. There was also some sadness and anger that she picked up on, and in one EVP, she captured a voice that stated: "You're so angry!"

As I ventured into the bell tower, I asked if anyone had died there and an EVP was recorded saying: "We don't know." Perhaps there are layers of spirits from different time periods that still roam or pass through the old firehouse and they too are unsure of its history.

With its long history and years of service, along with many generations of fireman, there are sure to be many remnants of emotions, hard work, and trying times that these dedicated community servicemen went through as they defended the town of Derry against destructive fires. These long-term memories and residual energy left behind from all these men, women, and events could surely be a contributing factor to possible paranormal activity at Halligan's. Many of the current fireman in the community have their own stories to tell of the Old Derry Firehouse. It was an interesting adventure for our team.

Meanwhile, for a great selection of draft beers (an outstanding feature at Halligan's), awesome food, and lively

Irish music in the bar that permeates the Tavern along with an overall friendly and appealing atmosphere, be sure to stop by. Perhaps Frank or some of the resident spirits will stop by and join you. Be sure to say thank you to Frank for his dedicated service to the community.

 The Halligan Tavern
32 W. Broadway
Derry, NH 03038
(603) 965-3490
halligantavern.com

10.

The Ghosts of the Windham Return
Windham, NH

The apparition (face) of a young boy at the Windham.
Photo courtesy of Leo Monfet

Everyone knows about the ghosts that frequent the Windham Restaurant in Windham, New Hampshire, but not everyone has the opportunity to conduct an investigation and interact with them. The owners were happy to have us and we brought along several special guests and the crew of the Hudson Cable

A quick streak of energy as the apparition of the young boy leaves.
Photo courtesy of Leo Monfet

Television Station (HDTV20 *Spectral Evidence*) to accompany us on our ghostly adventure there.

We set up several night-vision infrared cameras in the basement, which we learned from past encounters they usually show a great deal of paranormal activity. We let them roll while we made our way throughout the other rooms and three floors of the Windham. Psychic Medium April Sheerin was with the team tonight as well. It seems that whenever there is a medium present, it attracts activity from the ghostly residents. This was certainly the case this night. It was as if she had some type of magnetic pull on the Spirits. The fact that they know she senses them allows them to better communicate with us. For some ghosts, this may be all they need to help them to rest easier.

The Investigation Begins

In one of the dining rooms on the second floor, April sensed a man who had been severely burned on one half of his body. This had left him horribly scarred and disfigured. The accident had not been the cause of his demise, but his tragedy marred him for his entire life and he carried this with him to his grave. Because of his inability to resolve his sadness over this, he remains attached to the place where he befell the terrible experience.

While in the room making contact with this man, April said she felt as though she was on fire and the external temperature of the area around her went as high as 96 degrees according to our infrared and laser thermometers. Everywhere else in the room the temperature was a constant 70 degrees. It was only in the vicinity around April where the temperature spiked so high. Once contact was broken and she indicated that the ghost of this man had gone, the temperature around her fell to the same temperature as the rest of the room.

On the third floor, we experienced several entities. When my daughter and grandson, who accompanied us on this investigation, were in one of the rooms, we asked if this room had been someone's bedroom. We recorded an interactive EVP here saying: " Bedroom? Yes, I slept in here."

Neck and Neck

The ghosts of the Windham are generally very interactive and aware of our presence there. In one room on the third floor, my daughter felt extreme pain in her neck and a negative presence. Upon returning to the second floor, she said to me that her neck hurt badly and this had just started since going up to the third floor. We decided to have the entire team go up. In the room where my daughter had felt this negative presence and where she began feeling her neck hurt, April spoke up and, without ever having spoken to my daughter, said she felt a very strong and dark presence and that this entity had had a severe blow to the neck. My daughter and I made instant eye contact, as this certainly corroborated her same experience in this room.

Play Time

My grandson, Connor, sat down in a chair in the room and felt as though someone was pushing down on his shoulders. April said it was a little boy and that he wanted to play with Connor. It had been a long time since he had another little boy there to play with. April warned him that it was okay to come forward and speak and interact with us, but it was not okay for him to try and jump into Connor's body because he so missed having a physical body of his own. He seemed to then move away from surrounding Connor, but continued to interact with us throughout the night. I think he was happy to have someone his age there that evening.

Then April asked if they needed her to help them and a little child's voice was heard in an EVP message saying: "Yes, we need help." It is always emotional for us to hear these messages from little children, and try as we may to help them, it is not always effective for reasons we do not know.

History has told us that the Windham, built in the 1800s, was a tavern at one time. Before this, there was a farm on the land, as far back as the 1700s, and pioneers and Indians lived on the land. There are records of several deaths that occurred there and one of these was documented as a little boy who, we believe, is the boy who haunts the Windham. He was run over by a wagon in front of the building and passed away a short time after. A man who had a heart attack at the top of the stairs leading to the second floor and fell to his death down the stairs, has also been recorded.

Later, on the second floor, April sensed the spirits of several children, including the small boy. She told us that two young girls are always around him and they often protect him. During this time, the flashlight lit up and turned off several times in direct response to questions we asked of these ghostly children.

We closed out the investigation with a trip to the basement. April told us there were three loud and talkative spirits there. Two she knew were killed in this spot, but one was there for a reason other then the fact that he had died there. They had a sense of humor, she told us, and thought it was comical and curious that there were women in our group dressed in pants, because only men wore pants in their day. They perceived those of us wearing pants as being in our bloomers.

We captured several interesting anomalies in our video and infrared pictures. Our EVP were very evidential and characteristic of direct interaction with the ghosts of the Windham. Tune in to see the investigation when it airs on *Spectral Evidence* on Hudson Cable Television. There might be even more paranormal evidence for the show — we don't know about yet. After all, ghosts like to have their opportunity to smile for the camera, too!

 Windham Restaurant
59 Range Road
Windham, NH 03087
(603) 870-9270
windhamrestaurant.com

Here is the link to watch for the *Spectral Evidence* shows on HDTV20: www.hudsonctv.com/Cablecast/Public/Main.aspx?ChannelID=1

11.

A Private Home
Kingston, NH

Several members of the team, along with paranormal investigators from as far away as Connecticut and Maine, were invited to attend a fundraiser/paranormal investigation at a private residence in Kingston, New Hampshire. This residence was featured on an episode of Discovery Channel's *A Haunting*. The family has lived here for twenty-seven years. The story goes that the young family came to Kingston, New Hampshire, and found a home that was in much need of repair, but was a desirable location because of the many acres of land and a large barn it offered. The location seemed like the perfect place to start the kind of business they were thinking about. The husband was very handy at fixing things, so remodeling the old home was a challenge he was willing to undertake. The wife wanted to start a horse boarding and riding school and the land and barn would be very conducive to this business venture.

I was able to actually sit down with the owners of the home that Saturday, before the investigation, and have a personal interview with them. They told me that strange things began occurring on the property almost immediately after they moved in and were continuously happening. It began with a bicycle accident that happened to their young son. It was very serious but, fortunately, he was able to pull through okay. Additionally, lights would turn on and off in the house and the barn. The husband would thoroughly check the electrical connections and find nothing wrong. The horses would constantly be uneasy and get "spooked" by something in the middle of the night, disrupting the family's sleep, but there was never anything that could be found when they went to the barn to investigate the situation. Horse owners, riders, and students would complain that their horses were acting strangely and that they would feel uncomfortable every time they came onto the property. Some would sense that they were being watched and others had even been touched by something unseen.

Slowly, people began pulling their animals out of the business, and eventually, they had to close. The wife would tell her husband that she was always hearing voices, especially little children calling out "Mommy." The husband would experience strange happenings as well and he tried hard to dismiss them, but one day, when he and his wife were in the kitchen, he clearly heard the voice of an unseen child call out "Daddy!"

When they could no longer take it, they sought out many psychics and even a priest to try and help them, but many would not even consider the case and others could not affect the phenomena at all, no matter what they did to try to make it stop. Finally, they found a Shambala Healer and Master who agreed to face the challenge and try to help them.

A Shambala Healer

As she drove towards the home, she could already sense the presence of so many spirits from the long history and occupancy of the land. There was one strong and very negative male entity that she believed had kept slaves. He was a cruel and dominant person in life and was, she felt, the main reason for the negative energy the family was experiencing. It became her main focus to clear him from the property and restore good Karma to the home and the family.

The land was ancient. There had been many Indians who had lived and died on the land. Their energy remained there, but it was a peaceful and accepting energy. When the settlers came, many confrontations occurred. That residual energy remained. There was also a path through the woods on the property that had, in times long gone, served as a stagecoach road. Old coins had been found on the grounds along the path.

The land was heavily embedded with the energy of hundreds of spirits, but none of this seemed negative or confrontational to the Shambala Healer. Her main concern and focus was on ridding the property of the evil man. She felt that once he was gone, peace could again be restored to the family living there and to the spirits that remained with the land.

After performing the ritual clearing and banishment of this evil man's ghost, the paranormal activity seemed to become quieter. Normalcy slowly resumed and the negative feelings dissipated. The family began to once again feel safe.

Things do still happen, on occasion, but nothing threatening. The family has captured several interesting pieces of evidence, including the image of an Indian in the branches of an old historic apple tree on their property. One group in attendance that evening played an amazing EVP for me of the sounds of Indian chanting.

The activity on the land seems to be of a peaceful nature now and the family lives in harmony with their resident spirits. They have since opened a catering business and are happy to share their experiences with those, like us, whose passion is the study of the paranormal.

12.

Bucco's Tavern/Trattoria Al Bucco

Kingston, NH

"Pray for Me."

Strange anomaly in the basement of Bucco's Tavern. *Photo courtesy of Leo Monfet*

Buccos Tavern/Trattoria Al Bucco and restaurant once known as Rick's Café in Kingston, New Hampshire has always had a reputation for being haunted. There have been several name changes over the years, but this does not seem to be a problem for the spirits that haunt there. It's the history of this old building and the very long history of Kingston itself that lay reason to why it would naturally be haunted. We have done several investigations here in the past. Evidence of a haunting was always prevalent. A recent investigation yielded great paranormal evidence, including physical contact and paranormal audio and video captures.

The building was built in the 1700s, during the time of the Revolutionary War and America's struggle for independence. Kingston is one of the oldest and most historic towns in New Hampshire and the site of another well-known haunted and historic building, The Kingston 1686 House. This was the home of Josiah Bartlett who was one of the signers of the Declaration of Independence. He and his wife, Mary, and their twelve children lived here. It was a time of many struggles both from disease, Indian attacks, hard work, and the ensuing war for independence from Great Britain.

Strange anomaly in the attic. *Photo courtesy of Mike Sullivan*

The Investigation Begins

The first place we set up our equipment was in the attic area. We used infrared cameras, recorders, and motion sensors. April was drawn to one area of the attic. She felt a heavy sadness and sickening feeling there and told us that many people were quarantined and locked away there due to a smallpox epidemic. She said there were so many who succumbed to that traumatic disease in the location. One dominant man channeled through her and told her of the sadness and the many souls who became victims of smallpox. A very emotional EVP was captured here saying: "Pray for me." Perhaps it was this gentleman who told their tragic tale through April.

In every investigation we conduct, I go back and research the history of the area to further validate April's channeling abilities. She has never been wrong and the historical facts that I discover serve to validate her abilities even further. In letters written by Mary Bartlett to her husband, Josiah, she tells of the many deaths from a smallpox epidemic in the Kingston area. Further historical research also tells of the Great Throat Distemper that originated in Kingston in 1735 and resulted in the deaths of so many children and young adults. It started in Kingston and rapidly spread over areas all the way to Boston. Of those affected, almost all succumbed within days. April definitely has a direct line to the Otherside.

In the basement, Leo set up a new piece of equipment. This new laser device displays a kaleidoscope of mini-green pin-point lights that blanket the area. If anything interrupts this field of lights, it will clearly be seen. Both Regina and I observed a change in the pattern of the stream and consistency of the light pattern. A strange EVP was picked up here saying: "Pick a light." Were they manipulating the energy source to cause this light disruption?

Touch

At the same time, I was actually touched on the head by an unseen hand. It was so real I couldn't even speak for a moment. I was totally startled, but at the same time excited that I had just experienced actual physical contact. The touch sensation felt so very gentle rather then anything intense. April had sensed a young child that was hiding in the basement. Perhaps it was this little child who reached out to me. As we continued down into the basement, April picked up on several other entities that were present. When we asked how many were there with us, we captured an EVP saying: "There's seven."

With the long and, unfortunately, tragic history of this building, it is no wonder that there is so much residual energy left behind there. Kingston is one of the oldest and most historic towns in New Hampshire. After several very interesting investigations here, we have determined that Kingston is also one of the most haunted places in New Hampshire. It is a historical adventure to visit Kingston and there are wonderful places to dine, including this very haunted tavern. You can share a piece of history, some appetizers, and a brew at Buccos Tavern/Trattoria Al Bucco with, perhaps, one of its ghosts.

 Buccos Tavern/Trattoria Al Bucco
143 Main Street
Kingston, NH 03848
(603) 642-4999

> While in the area, also check out the haunted Kingston 1686 House. This was the home of Josiah Bartlett who was one of the signers of the Declaration of Independence. He and his wife, Mary, and their twelve children lived here. It was a time of many struggles both from disease, Indian attacks, hard work, and the ensuing war for independence from Great Britain. (Read more about the Kingston House in my first volume of *Spooky Creepy New England!*)

13.
The Laconia State School
Laconia, NH

The Laconia State School was a product of the times and conditions of society in the late 1800s and early 1900s. It was founded in 1901 and opened in 1903, with the intent of creating a place for the poor and indigent who were placed in poor houses and on poor farms. Society at the time, then went further to label these people as "feebleminded," and deemed them social outcasts. Those who did not fit the norms due to something as minute as stuttering, spasms, epilepsy, or even simply being poor and uneducated, would be reason enough to gain entrance to an institution. The original intention of this school may have been well meaning, but its final result was deplorable. In the end, there was no separation on the basis of the severity of one's disability and with extreme overcrowding and deterioration of conditions, the identities and character of these poor souls were lost in chaos and uncaring.

All of this came to an end when, through reform for those with disabilities, the Laconia State School finally shut its doors in 1991. But the residual energy of the suffering and sorrow that existed there permeates the halls and walls of these now-silent structures. Perhaps the ghosts of the many trapped souls who died there and lie buried in the nearby cemetery may still be reliving this horror and, sadly, are unable to move on. If you have the chance to visit, listen closely for the sounds of shuffling feet across the floor and the screams and cries for help and comfort in the echoes of this deserted place.

In 1903, the school housed around sixty women, ages 3 to 21. The age limit expanded to 45, several years later. But with every passing decade, the numbers grew to hundreds more and began including both male and female, adults and children all mixed in together. Then further inhumanity against residents came about when laws were enacted that made residents, most of them younger women, undergo mandatory sterilization, so that they could not reproduce. If it was determined that a patient was to be released back into society, sterilization was a definite condition of that release.

During and after the years of the Great Depression and ensuing wars, more and more people were institutionalized in Laconia and, at its peak, there were over 1,000 patients all crowded into these small spaces. Sanitation and disease became a major problem. The stench would have been nauseating. Because the institution was so understaffed, patients lacked care and were simply left unattended, some just lying on the cold and drafty floor. There were reported cases of extreme physical, sexual, verbal, and emotional abuse. Shock treatment therapy, icy-cold water baths, and beatings were common place as ways to handle the uncontrollable. Patients were heavily drugged and bound in straitjackets for additional restraint. Little children were made to work for long hours in physically intensive jobs and paid pennies an hour. Their money and possessions were stolen. Violence amongst the patients was rampant and many were marked with bruises, cuts, and scratches showing the signs of these attacks. Whatever condition these unfortunate souls were suffering from was most certainly exacerbated by their incarceration within the walls of this dreadful place.

By the 1970s and 1980s, the population of the Laconia State School began to decline as the local and federal governments intervened to stop the horrific treatment of the developmentally disabled in institutions throughout the nation. Those remaining residents were slowly acclimated back into society and into community programs. The school closed its doors in 1991, but the suffering and torments that happened there are carved forever in this place and cast a dark and dirty smudge on human history.

Laconia Cemetery

Nearby in Meredith, New Hampshire, along Chemung Road, is the Laconia Cemetery. It is the final resting place of over 160 former residents of the Laconia State School. The graves were once unmarked and the names of those poor souls would have forever been lost in time. But through the help of relatives and friends, the names and lifelines of those who lived and died at the school have been identified and their dignity has once again been restored. May they finally rest in Peace, free from further harm.

An Investigation

Some of the team members had the privilege of doing an investigation at the former Laconia State School. They were allowed admission to several of the buildings. Leo was able to capture some interesting images on infrared and Rocky recorded some startling video. Everyone felt a strong sense of emotional residual energy at the location. This was an interesting and profound investigation for the team. An opportunity to investigate a place with so much history reminiscent of a period in time where those who were considered social outcasts because of mental deficiencies were incarcerated and, more often than not, victims of neglect and abuse is every paranormal researcher's desire. The spirits of the Laconia State School just can't seem to let go and move on. They lack the happiness everyone in life deserves to have from time to time and the fulfillment of life itself. And so they wander on aimlessly and timelessly in the halls of the only place they knew as home.

 The Laconia State School
The Laconia State Cemetery
Chemung Road
Meredith Center
Meredith, NH 03253

Note that although the police use part of this location, it is private property.

14.
A Haunting in a Private Residence
Derry, NH

It was said that a young child of about four years of age was abducted from her bed in her nightclothes and bare feet by her uncle during the late 1800s. The uncle, a mentally disturbed man, smothered the small child. Upon realizing what he had done, he panicked and ran, holding her lifeless body in his arms. In his confession, he told of how he buried her body beneath a tree somewhere in the woods. When cross-examined, he had slipped even more into insanity and could not remember the location of her body. Her parents were also held negligent for not reporting her missing for more then two days. Although a search was conducted, the poor little girl's remains were never found. So, she roams as a ghostly apparition, looking for resolution, perhaps not even realizing she is dead. This is the story that brings us to this haunted investigation.

Everyone Sees

Three generations of psychics live in this Derry home: the grandmother, mother, and daughter. All have experienced phenomena in the home. The family has lived in the home for eighteen years and has experienced phenomena on and off throughout that time. The other children living there have also had experiences, although not to the degree as the mother and daughter. The young daughter has been seeing and hearing the apparition of a small child wearing a white nightgown and having bare feet since she herself was a little girl. She told us the ghost often hums and whispers in her ear. There have been instances of decorations flying off the shelves in the kitchen and smashing on the floor and a family picture, firmly fastened to the wall above the fireplace, that simply comes off the wall and lands several feet across the room on the living room floor with no glass breakage, but the frame completely disassembled. It is as if it had been lifted off of the wall and placed upon the floor by unseen hands. This has happened not just once, but on many occasions and always in the same fashion. The family cats seem to stare at emptiness that human eyes cannot see and sounds of whispers emanate from nowhere.

There is no sense among the owners of unhappiness or anything negative and they have come to live with the occurrences as a regular thing, but they sought information from us through whatever evidence we might gather that would, perhaps, help them find out who the spirits were. Is the little girl the spirit of the child who was murdered? She appeared to the daughter exactly as she was described in the story about the crime: in a white nightdress with no shoes on her feet.

The mother told us that one day when she was at home and upstairs she heard the sounds of heavy footsteps coming up the basement stairs when there was no one home but her. She said she was so frightened and thought someone had broken into the house. The sound soon dissipated, and when she went through the house, there was no sign of anyone having come in or having been in the home. Everything was as it was and completely undisturbed. Who then was this entity? Certainly the tiny steps of a four-year-old spirit could not have caused such loud thumping.

The owners have felt the presences of several spirits in their home. Interestingly, we later captured an EVP, after Rocky had asked, " How many spirits are in this house?" that replied: "Seven?"

The younger son, whose bedroom was on the second floor, had once called his mother because he could not sleep. He told her there were people looking at him, walking around the room, laughing and dancing. The Mother saw no one at that moment, but on many other occasions had heard the exact same voices and sounds. On one occasion, as she entered the living room, she saw a woman sitting in the chair and singing to a little baby she held in her arms. She then vanished in the blink of an eye.

Rocky and I went up to the upstairs bedroom where the boys slept, sat down upon the beds and attempted to record messages. Other then Leo, who was standing in the doorway to the room taking infrared photographs, there was no one else present in the room with us. At this time, while I was sitting down on the bed, I asked the question, "Can you please show yourself for us in a picture?" Upon review of Leo's pictures, and to our amazement, the image of a young woman, obscured partially by a white cloud of misty energy, appeared standing near the table against the wall behind Rocky and me. No one in the house recognized her as being anyone they knew or had ever seen. As mentioned, we were the only people in the room, and furthermore, there was nowhere she could have been standing behind us. The beds were against the wall and in-between them was the table. Rocky and I sat on the ends of each bed. Who then was this entity that came through for us in such a clear manifestation in Leo's photograph? This was one of the clearest images I have yet seen. We were all in somewhat a state of shock and no matter how hard we tried to explain it away, we could not. She was there. It should be further noted that there was an instant drop in temperature as when we entered that room. It is documented that entities seem to pull from the heat energy in the environment to manifest.

While recording in the downstairs bedroom, Rocky, Leo, and I all heard two very pronounced knocks coming from outside the window. The owner had previously told us they all sensed a presence in the backyard. Circumstances due to the icy weather and because it was pitch black outside made it impractical for us to go out and investigate the source of the knocks. It was highly improbable anyway that someone would have been out there in those conditions and in the dark knocking on windows. Yet all of us heard the sound clearly coming from the outside of the window. Later, the same sound was verified in the video and EVP recordings that were running at the time of the occurrence.

Rocky also captured a large mist of energy behind Leo as we were in the lower-level bedroom and several streaks of what looked like ectoplasm energy appearing in many of the infrared photographs taken there. The K2 meter responded by lighting up on several occasions while in the daughter's bedroom in the basement. While asking questions, the meter lit up all the lights as if indicating a high EMF (electromagnetic field), which is often prevalent when Spirit energy is near. We all believed it might have been the little girl's presence. It happened only a few times and then stopped, as if whatever energy was there had left.

We were able to pick up some very relevant EVP messages during the investigation. In one of my recordings, a male voice is heard in what sounds like: "Little girl's missing." In two other recordings, we hear what sounds like a child's voice crying out, but the gist of the message is hard to decipher. One significant and interactive EVP capture followed Rocky asking, "Are you buried in the backyard?" and an eerie and disembodied voice answering: "I don't knoooooow!"

We heard from the same little voice once again in an EVP when asked if they liked the children who lived in the house. The reply sounds like: "I do."

One rather humorous EVP was captured after I made repeated inquires of the Spirits in the home. I assume they had had enough of my questioning and replied in an EVP: "That's all you get!"

It is a common practice of ours to introduce ourselves on investigations. It is part of the respectability we show to Spirit when conducting a case. Leo, Rocky, and I were first to arrive and so we introduced ourselves on the recorder. Mike arrived a short time later, and when he began his EVP recordings, he was immediately greeted, without ever stating his name, with an EVP saying: "Michael Sullivan," and then another later saying: "Michael and Mike." Theory has it that telepathic ability exists in the Spirit world so they must have known through thought transfer who Mike was immediately when he arrived.

With all the evidence we have compiled from this investigation, we were invited back to review it with the homeowners and family. It is likely that several positive spirits haunt this house, in our opinion. We feel as though this is a very safe home and the Karma is very gentle and inviting. The entities there are of a positive nature and nothing threatening exists in this beautiful home. The family has lived with these phenomena for many years and accepted this. They merely sought validation, if possible, for whom these spirits were. We believe our evidence can help provide some of the answers, but much will still remain a mystery because those who roam there will likely keep to themselves.

I only hope that somehow the death of this little girl can be resolved, and that at some space and time, she can find her way to the Otherside to be rejoined with her family and the ones who so love her.

15.

A Haunted Video Store
Windham, NH

Our investigation brought us to a video store in the local area that had reported several paranormal happenings. The shop had been home to several other businesses before it became a video store. One of the owners reported that he had, on several occasions, been working in the store alone and heard the sounds of a group of people making a lot of noise in one of the adjoining rooms. He said that it sounded like there was a party going on. They had also come into the store one day and witnessed DVDs that had flown off the shelf and landed over ten feet away, as if thrown the distance by a powerful unseen force.

The Investigation Begins

With all of this having been told to us, we were anxious to see if any of this paranormal activity would play out while we conducted an investigation there. So, equipped with our usual bundle of paranormal equipment—infrared cameras, digital recorders, EMF meters, video cameras, and digital temperature gauges—we began the adventure. Arriving at 8 p.m., we gathered and set up our equipment. Then it was lights out and we started the investigation. The main part of the store was not that large and so easily manageable. We could always see where the members of the team were, so we did not need to concentrate on keeping together. There were basically three areas. I felt most of the activity occurred in the room directly facing the main lobby and entrance. There was a small black curtain hanging in the room which swayed gently every time you passed by it. Nothing paranormal, but it certainly helped enhance the effect of a supposedly haunted store.

Upon first arriving, Carrie lent me her copper dowsing rods, so that we could try to make an initial connection with whomever the Spirit(s) present were. In this dowsing, I asked the Spirit to cross the rods for a *yes* answer and to spread them apart for a *no* answer. I then proceeded to ask several questions.

"Are you a man?" The reply was *no*. Naturally, this leaves only one other option; the communicating ghost was a woman. So we wondered if there were other spirits there. But when this question was proposed, the rods did not cross. This was an indication that she was the only one. We continued with the questions, trying to figure out how old she might be: "over 40?" *No.* Then "under 40?" *Yes.* Carrie guessed 35 years old. *No.* Rocky guessed 37 and 38. *No.* I guessed 31 and the rods crossed to a *yes* answer. So now we knew that we were in contact with a woman that was 31 years old and that she was the dominant Spirit present there.

We continued with a few other questions with the rods, asking if we were wanted there; if she wanted us to leave; why she was there and whether or not we could help her. All through this interrogation the rods fluctuated between strong affirmative and negative or indecisive responses. Carrie felt as though the rods were actually pulling away from her and sometimes pulling strongly downward. Interestingly, JW asked the question: "Did you die here?" and the rods almost instantly crossed to a very strong *yes*. Through this dowsing, we were able to ascertain many facts about our resident ghost. Now we began zeroing in on responses more detailed then *yes* or *no* replies through the inception of EVP.

With recorders in hand, Mike, Karen, and JW began asking questions and requests of the Spirit of the lady. In conjunction with us recording, Leo was taking infrared shots. Carrie, JW, and Mike were taking digital pictures and video. Carrie took a shot where an interesting energy mass was seen in one spot of the room, preceded by a white streak of what looked liked ectoplasm stretching out in front of it across the floor. In the very next shot, it had moved clear across the room. In another photo Carrie took, there was a large misty form of energy right on me as I was walking out of the room. Was this lady spirit following me?

I have a tendency to be very empathic in investigations and sense the emotions of those who may tragically or otherwise be earthbound and remain trapped in a place due to some form of trauma or emotion that may have occurred in the time of their physical life. We always try to be respectful and never force or demand answers from the entity(s). We asked if she could move something to show us that she was there or to make a knocking sound for us. Nothing happened in response to this request. It is my opinion that free will exists in the Spirit world, just like it does here in the physical. You can't make a spirit do what you ask, and antagonizing them doesn't work every time either, nor is it our practice to conduct our investigations this way. I sometimes push a little further to say such things as: "We would appreciate it if you could move something and can't be sure if you are really here unless you show us," though I know our photos, videos, and EVP are the main evidence that will later reveal the presence of spirit and paranormal activity.

Before finishing up the investigation for the night, we played several of our EVP back and it was clear that we had captured many responses on our recorders. We would be able to interpret these messages more clearly when we analyzed the evidence from the investigation. Before we left the store, we did one final EVP thanking whoever came through for us that evening. This is something we always do when closing out the night. We also thanked our host for allowing us the opportunity to come in for this paranormal adventure. Since there were surveillance cameras in the store, we suggested he examine tapes to see if the security cameras had picked up anything that could validate the paranormal occurrences that had previously been reported there.

A Parting Answer

When I got home that evening, I played back a few of the EVP I had recorded during the investigation. One interesting message came through and was heard right off the recorder very clearly. I had asked the Spirit of the lady why she remained there and if she was tied to the business. I received this reply: "Please...no one cares about me."

I felt so sad when I heard this and can only wonder what may have occurred in this woman's life to make her feel so alone and unappreciated. This is part of the reason we are driven so passionately to paranormal research and our findings: first to validate that something truly exists after the change of physical death and that energy continues in some form, and second, to try to establish a consistency in our findings that can help us understand why strong emotion tends to so often be exhibited in cases of what we refer to as "haunting."

16.
My Hudson Haunted Houses
Hudson, NH

Misty sees the Spirit. *Photo Karen Mossey*

I often wonder whether all four different houses I lived in while in Hudson, New Hampshire, haunted or was it me that brought about the paranormal occurrences that happened in every one of them? I thought I would relate my haunted happenings in these homes to you.

House One

We moved to the United States from Germany in 1964, buying a 1950s house whose previous owner had died. He had not died *in* the house but his widow, who sold us the house, said he loved the home and was always very attached to it. I remember sitting up late and watching TV on several nights and I would hear the piano start playing in the living room. I was too scared to get up and see if it may have been one of my brothers or sisters, but they didn't play the piano and I knew they were all either in bed or not at home. It happened quite often.

Then there was the time, during daylight hours, I came in from swimming in the pool and as I took the corner from the kitchen and entered the dining room, I saw a white figure in a bathrobe float right across the doorway and vanish into the wall. My father worked the graveyard shift, so he slept during the day. At first I thought he had gotten up to go to the bathroom as I tried to rationalize what I had just seen. As quickly as I had seen whatever it was, it was gone. I ran up the stairs and peeked into my mother and father's room and Dad was sleeping soundly in his bed.

House Two

We moved to the other end of town as I grew older. My father and husband renovated an old cottage and we moved in. It was one of the first houses in Hudson and had been owned by the Ford family. The Fords were some of the original settlers from Hudson. We were told a man died on the property while they were blasting for a well. I can't say, without a doubt, that this is true, but that is what we heard. The house had several spooky things happen. I would often be home alone and the rocking chair in the living room would start moving back and forth all by itself. Then, one night, I woke up out of a deep sleep and saw a dark, shadowy figure sitting on top of me and holding me down. I was so scared, but I grabbed a hold of my courage and shut my eyes and wished it away. When I opened my eyes, it was gone. I only experienced that once. Scientists have attributed this to a condition called sleep paralysis or "The Old Hag Syndrome." But to me, it was much too real to have been my imagination.

House Three

My third house was a condex and was relatively new when we moved in. Both the kids, my friends who visited, and I all had very frightening experiences living in this home. When we first moved in, I found all sorts of metaphysical books left in the basement. There were several strange books on the subject of the paranormal and supernatural. Perhaps the previous owners were also experiencing things in this home.

One of the first things to happen was both of my sons experienced seeing people walking around. On several occasions, my son, Alex, would tell me he could not sleep at night because there were always people walking around in his room. One time we were playing together with his soldiers downstairs and he asked me to go and get his disco ball upstairs. I said, "Why don't you go get it yourself?" He ran to the stairs, gazed up, and then ran back over to me and said, "Mom, can you go get it?" I asked why and he said, "Because those people are standing at the top of the stairs." I went over to the stairs and looked, but saw no one. I went up and got his toy and brought it down.

Then, one evening when I came home from work, he ran over to me and told me that he had seen one of the ladies, dressed all in a white dress, sitting on the edge of my bed. I asked him if she was friendly and he said she just looked at him and did not speak.

My son, Sean, always closed his bedroom door tight at night. I asked him why and he said that he saw things and shadows move by his door when it was open. He told me they were darker than dark and he could see them against the black of night. He didn't want them in his room. One time, he told me, one of them came in and pushed him up against the wall.

Also, my older daughter, Jessica, explained to me how she was walking up the stairs and could hear someone following her so closely that she could feel breathing on her neck. But when she turned around, there was nothing there. Why was I not seeing them and everyone else was?

Perhaps the best validation to corroborate all the children's experiences was when my good friend, Kevin, visited me and stayed over one night. We were sitting at the dining room table talking and drinking a beer together. We were talking about our loved ones who had passed on. The children were watching TV in the living room. As I finished my beer, I heard an ear-piercing shrill sound and the bottom of my glass sheared right off and fell into my hand. There were no sharp edges. It was as though a laser had cut right through it. Kevin and I looked at one another and strongly felt the presence of something unexplainable.

The next morning, Kevin took a shower and when he came downstairs he looked at me and said, "Karen, are you selling your house?" I told him that I was not. He then asked why then were all those people walking around upstairs. I looked at him dumfounded. He said a few of them were carrying clipboards. I went upstairs and saw nothing.

Over the next couple of days the house flooded with flies. There were so many of them that even all the fly strips we had could not keep them under control. It was so awful, we could not stay there. When we came back several hours later, they were all gone or dead.

What was going on? That evening I went to sleep and woke up to a freezing cold presence near my bed. The clock had stopped at 2 a.m. I thought maybe there had been a power outage, so I went downstairs to check the time on the other clocks. None of them had stopped. They were all working perfectly. The only one that had stopped and was blinking at 2 a.m. was mine and it had happened right when the room became so cold.

We moved out of that house and I often wonder if the couple that bought it has had similar experiences.

House Four

The final house in Hudson also had its share of paranormal goings on. When my good friend, Debby, visited me, she told me she believed the house to have very good Karma. I have to admit, I never had a bad paranormal encounter there, although I had several experiences. I would often hear people talking at the foot of my bed while I was half asleep. Once, I let my recorder run for awhile before going to sleep and I asked if there were any messages for me. An EVP voice was heard on playback saying: "Quiet down...Be quiet...I'm trying to sleep!" Other then the dog lying at the foot of my bed there was absolutely no one in the room but me.

Then I had a student stay with me for awhile and she would often tell me that she saw a bright light come into the basement where she was sleeping and then see a young girl and man talking together. She told me they seemed to be talking about the cat that was sleeping in the chair. She said she was too afraid to move and pulled the blankets up over her head.

The dog would often bark down in the basement at things I certainly could not see. I once spoke out loud and said, "Well, whoever you are, thank you for visiting." The dog suddenly stopped his barking. Perhaps it was one of my loved ones who was just dropping by and wanted to be acknowledged.

I remember once watching my cat, Misty, meowing continuously and looking all around in my bedroom. She stared up at the ceiling as if she was looking at something and then followed it all over the room. She jumped up on the window sill and looked into the window. I quickly snapped a picture and what I saw in the photo was a figure that looked something like a human and an owl reflected from inside my room into the window glass. It freaked me out. I had not seen this creature in my room but Misty surely had and followed it around.

I have since moved to Nashua and, other than the ghostly cat that rooms the attic, I have had no experiences. My sons and my son's girlfriend have, however, saying they have often seen an older man. Everything is quiet and the feeling is positive. I still often wonder. Is it because I work with those in spirit so often that I am more open to these occurrences? Is it truly the houses that are haunted or is it really me?

17.

Eggie's Diner
Atkinson, NH

Eggie's diner is haunted. There is little doubt about that. The evidence captured was totally conclusive that several ghosts exist there. They also seem pretty adamant about staying. Even the staff is a little leery about trying to persuade them to move on. Perhaps having a good breakfast with a ghost or two may attract clientele to Eggie's. Experiencing such an encounter is the reason we were brought into this investigation.

Eggie's Diner. *Photo courtesy of Mike Sullivan*

An Investigation Begins

Accompanying us on this case was Psychic Medium April Sheerin. It is almost a sure bet that something out of the ordinary will occur when April is with us. The entities sense her presence and know that they will be noticed. April can connect with them. It's hard to imagine what it is like being in their world. They continue to exist freely in this parallel dimension noticed by one another in their ethereal realm, but unnoticed by those of us in the physical, except for on rare occasions. When the two dimensions come close enough and the vibration is such that they can prove their presence by moving something or manifesting a message through EVP, we realize that we are in the presence of ghosts. At times, they have shown up as an apparition visible to all or on camera, video, or infrared film. Such was the case at Eggie's.

April felt there were several ghostly presences there. Almost immediately upon entering the diner she knew that the ghost of a crotchety, older man was present. His energy was quite strong. She was going to attempt to persuade him to move on, but the staff advised against it. They thought it would make him even more angry and disruptive. In an EVP, April stated, "Oh, they are going to be sorry they don't cross this one over." The male spirit followed her statement with a bold profanity. She also sensed the presence of a woman at this same time. She said she saw her wearing an apron and that she was not very old, but not young either—and quite spry. At this time, I captured a very clear EVP of a woman's voice saying: "Hello?" It was as if she was sensing our presence but confused about what was happening.

We believe the minute we turn on these digital recorders a static disruption in the vibration can be sensed in the ethereal dimension where the spirits reside and they can feel this. It's like picking up a phone or answering the door and not knowing who or what is there. The voice was only heard on the recording and did not appear on our video which was running at the same time. This is because ghosts can only manipulate one energy source at a time in most cases. The same EVP will almost never appear on two sources at the same time.

Disruptions

Eggie's had undergone several renovations. This can often disrupt the ghosts. They are used to going about their business in the environment that they lived in when they were physically alive. The staff had already had several strange things happen during regular business hours. Customers were experiencing strange phenomena.

On one occasion, we were told a family was having breakfast when their daughter's eating utensil was pulled out of her hand. They were totally startled at what had just happened.

It is said that the main dining area, which was recently remodeled, is where most of the activity occurs. The waitstaff believes it to be the older man. April corroborated this. She said he is the strongest presence there and very grumpy.

We were also told of at least two deaths, a man and a woman, that had occurred in the diner when it was a private home. April also sensed that there was a great deal of energy present on the land itself that went back hundreds of years. She felt the presences of colonial settlers and many American Indians.

When we went down into the basement, several of the team felt as though they were touched. At one point, we felt as though we were being taunted by the ghosts there. Things were shutting on and off and there was so much commotion that April actually got angry and said, "You're not very funny. I am not impressed anymore!" Of course, the ghost followed that up with a loud and mean: "Damn you," and then later: "Get out!"

April sensed many struggles by early inhabitants. She said they were telling her that they were very cold and were always in need of more wood to keep themselves warm. Later, upon review of our evidence, in an EVP captured in the basement, two spirits confirmed what April had previously sensed. A male spirit states: "We don't have the wood to burn." This is followed by a second ghostly voice replying: "I'll go and get some." I wonder if they are they still going through the struggles of their daily lives as it was during the time they were physically alive? It would seem so.

Our night concluded with a séance in the main dining room where we had previously sensed the strong presence of the dominant male ghost and the spry, middle-aged woman with an apron on. April concluded that, in addition to several adult spirit entities, there were also children present. She felt, however, that the children were not trapped ghosts, as were the man and the woman, but rather that they came in to visit now and then to the place where they had many memories. We felt honored that they came to visit when we were there. They were playful and seemed to enjoy turning the flashlight on and off several times.

With the long-term occupancy of this residence, combined with the energy left on the land itself, it is no wonder Eggie's diner is haunted.

I think the lure of perhaps having a ghostly encounter and the fact that the breakfast is exceptional and the coffee is wonderful, makes Eggie's Diner in Atkinson a popular place to go and enjoy. Just be sure to get a good grasp on your fork and spoon. Seems the ghosts are hungry, too. Have fun!

 Eggie's Diner
6 Main Street
Atkinson, NH 03811
(603) 489-1858
http://eggiesfamilyrestaurant.com/

Maine

18.

The Spinney's of Kittery, ME

Spiney Tombstone. *Photo courtesy of Cynthia Wrocklage*

I visited my sister in Kittery, Maine, in early November. It was a long, overdue trip that I had been looking forward to. She moved into a lovely home overlooking the Pascataqua River. You can see the bridge connecting New Hampshire and Maine and the lights of neighboring Portsmouth through her living room window. The view is spectacular! The home has a long history and the land it sits upon is even more ancient. She told me that on the land to the side of her home are some old gravestones in a family burial ground belonging to the Spinney family. In days of long ago, families buried their loved ones on the land near their homestead.

The cemetery was the first place she brought me to when I arrived at her house. As we approached, I sensed a very strong energy of little children and I turned to her and said, "Oh my gosh, there are little babies buried in here."

As we approached the first stone, she turned and looked at me with paleness on her face.

"Kare," she said. "How did you know?"

The stone that stood before us was that of an infant child only fourteen days old. Children's energy is different from that of adults. You can feel it in the depths of your stomach as you approach. It is not a heaviness, but rather a light and delicate, almost Angelic, energy of a pure and innocent soul.

There are several graves in the tiny plot of land. Some of them were hard to read, dating back to the 1700s. Others were toppled over or only part of the original stone remained. A short distance from one burial area was another family plot. This one was surrounded by a very old and rusted wrought-iron gate that was chained and locked. The name Spinney was on the entrance gateway. I would like to go again in the spring and summer when the weather is better and the night's stay lighter longer and glance further inside this cemetery.

The Spinney name goes as far back as the year 1066. It had several different spellings. The original settlers came from England to Nova Scotia and then immigrated down along the Pascataqua River to Eliot and Kittery, Maine. They owned many hundreds of acres of land along the river and on each side of Great cove which was eventually named "Spinneys Cove."

I always like to know more about the lives of the family members that lie at rest in these cemeteries. I researched further into the history

Josiah Spinney. *Photo courtesy of
Cynthia Wrocklage*

of the Spinney families of Kittery, Maine. The Spinneys were some of the original settlers in Kittery. John Spinney was born in Kittery, Maine, on July 17, 1691. He lived his entire life in Kittery and died on the 4th of July in 1726, at the young age of only 35. He married Patience Shepard and they had five children: Anne, Zebulen, Johannah, Sheepherd, and Elizabeth. So began the legacy of seven generations of Spinneys. Their descendants remain in large numbers as residents of Kittery to this day.

There are also many stories about the Spinney brothers as great fishermen in Kittery. They worked hard all their lives and lived to be in their 90s. One legend tells of how one of the brothers, David, in the last years of his life, had pure white hair. As the story goes, all of his hair fell out of his head and pure black hair proceeded to grow in until the day he passed on.

The Spinneys lived out their lives in small cottages along the river. During the early days of settlers, there was the constant threat of Indian attacks and life was not easy for these early pioneers. Children and women were often kidnapped by the Indians and sold to the French who held them for ransom for money or land. Most of the settlers were poor and could not afford the cost. Letters were often written to higher authorities to plead for the return of their families. But through all the hard times, these people loved the land and the waters and Kittery became and is today the home of many generations of Spinneys.

The land my sister's home is built upon was part of the original Spinney homestead and several generations of Spinneys are buried on this land. This old burial ground near my sister's home is a great historical treasure. It is a testament to the legacy, lives, and losses of the Spinney families of Kittery, Maine. The Karma I felt there was a very good one. These were good, hearty, and hardworking people who, despite their many struggles, persevered and loved their home. Perhaps they still stop by, on occasion, to visit my sister in her wonderful abode. I believe they would approve of all the beautiful work she and her husband and family have done to restore their home.

Connecticut

19.
The New London Ledge Lighthouse
Groton, CT

New London Ledge Lighthouse in the fog. *Photo courtesy of Leo Monfet*

Inside the Lighthouse. *Photo courtesy of Leo Monfet*

I had the opportunity to join in on an overnight investigation at the New London Ledge Lighthouse in Groton, Connecticut. We were accompanied by a television Producer/Director and his camera crew who were doing a documentary for *The American Builder* television show. The Director, and the episode of The New London Ledge Lighthouse, later, won an Emmy for this documentary: episode 04E15 (Season 4, Episode 15). This paranormal investigation and the evidence we gathered was truly solid proof of many strange and unusual supernatural occurrences that happened at this unique and very historic lighthouse.

We arrived in Groton early in the day and were taken by boat over to the lighthouse where we were dropped off for our investigation. The boat would not be coming back to retrieve us until the following morning. It was very exciting knowing we would be left alone, out in the middle of the harbor, overnight, in a very haunted three-story high lighthouse. We had packed up water, food, blankets and, most important, all of our paranormal equipment. It was a calm, seasonably mild day but being on the water and in a haunted place will always make it feel so much colder. Our adrenaline was pumping and we were all really anxious for this incredible adventure.

This amazing lighthouse was built in 1909 to serve as a guide to warn ships and their crews of the ledges in the Thames River near the mouth of New London Harbor at Groton, Connecticut. The lighthouse was manned by lighthouse keepers and the Coast guard up until it became automated in 1987.

The New London Ledge lighthouse does not resemble an ordinary light house, but a one-of-a-kind-looking structure that resembles a Victorian-style brick building with three floors. It is fifty-two square feet and thirty-four feet high—this is an ominous building. Inside are bedrooms, staircases, a kitchen, and architecture of a large, stately home. The tower, which houses the Fresnel lens, adorns the top of the building.

Many a lighthouse keeper and coast guard crewman reported having had paranormal encounters in the building. Some of these experiences included doors opening and slamming shut, lights turning on and off, blankets being whisked off the beds at night, objects being moved or misplaced and reappearing in other locations, and ghostly voices being heard throughout the lighthouse. Some members of the coast guard crew who staffed the lighthouse

The author on the Lighthouse. *Photo courtesy of Leo Monfet*

experienced chills and cold spots on even the warmest of evenings. Others making their rounds were said to have heard knocks and thumps throughout the night. Oftentimes, electronic devices and even the television sets would turn on and off by themselves.

So, with the fog settling in upon us, our equipment set up and ready to go, we headed into our investigation of this very foreboding and spooky place. No one planned to sleep at all that night. The camera crew was rearing to go and followed us from room to room. We set up some trigger objects in some of the rooms and marked the area where we had placed them with a chalk line. This way if the object moved from its original location, we could determine this. Everyone kept together so we could make sure no one moved anything. Investigating the inside of the building would be our first mission. Later, we would head outside and walk the perimeters of the lighthouse.

Everyone had heard the story of the ghost called "Ernie." Legend has it that he threw himself to his death from on top of the lighthouse. The story goes that his wife grew tired of long and lonely nights and that she ran off with a sailor. Devastated and

Outside the Lighthouse. *Photo courtesy of Leo Monfet*

seeing no other option, "Ernie" plummeted to his demise. Because his business remained unfinished and his death traumatic, Ernie could not rest in peace. He was doomed to endlessly haunt the lighthouse. His paranormal escapades have frightened many of the former staff and investigators.

During the investigation, we were also told the story of a boat that capsized in the strong currents surrounding the lighthouse. The boat was manned by a father, mother, and their young teenage daughter. They were out for a leisurely boat ride on a calm and sunny day when a storm suddenly came up. They found themselves drifting further and further out into the harbor and could not get back to the shore. The currents were too strong and kept pulling them back out. The boat eventually capsized and was found empty when it washed up along the shore. The keeper of the lighthouse, at the time, said that a man and a woman had come up the stairs to the lighthouse that night. They were soaking wet and did not speak a word. He helped them up and went to get dry garments and blankets. When he came back they were gone and there was no trace of them ever seen again. A person walking along the shore also noticed a young woman who was wearing a wet dress walking along the sand of the beach. He turned to call out to her and she vanished in front of his eyes. No bodies were ever found. It cannot be verified that either "Ernie" existed, or the three others were the ghosts of the boat crash.

Séances and EVPs

Lighthouses are notoriously known to be haunted. Each has its own legends and ghostly tales. As paranormal investigators, we like to think these stories are true, especially considering some of the phenomenal evidence we captured at this one on this night.

Inside the stately lighthouse, we conducted a few séances. We captured voices of children on our digital recorders and a strong gruff male voice telling us to "Get out." One of the most remarkable EVPs occurred on the outside of the lighthouse. I was standing near the steps where, as legend has it, a man and woman from the capsized boat were helped up by the light keeper. I turned on the recorder and asked if there was anyone out there with me? On playback, I heard a bone-chilling EVP of a woman saying: "Help me, I'm cold." Being rather empathic myself, I could not help but feel the despair from this woman's voice.

The fog completely wrapped around the lighthouse which made the atmosphere very eerie. In the distance, you could hear the sound of music and laughter from the nightclubs on the shore. I can imagine how these happy sounds would upset a lonely ghost out at the lighthouse. They are trapped there. These earthbound souls must roam endlessly in the place of their tragic end. Psychics have gone to the lighthouse and have attempted to help them move on, but it is my opinion that unless a ghost wants to go, there is no force on Earth that can make them.

The investigation of the New London Ledge Lighthouse was an incredible adventure and yielded very strong evidence that left me with no doubt that the place was indeed haunted.

 ## The New London Ledge Lighthouse

Located on the Thames River, with entrance to New London Harbor. The closest city is Groton. Info@LedgeLighthouse.org

Project Oceanology offers tours and events at this incredible lighthouse in July and August each year. More information can be found at the website www.oceanology.org/lighthouse.html.

Paranormal Stuff

20

History and the Paranormal

Once in awhile, we hear of paranormal phenomena in brand new or newer structures. Theory has it that this can be attributed to many factors, some of which are:

LOCATION:

a). Is the structure on land where previous dwellings existed and some of this long-term energy remains behind?

b). Was the structure built on granite, limestone, or perhaps where Ley lines cross? These elements have been shown to have high EMF, which are thought to be conducive to enhancing paranormal activity, whether caused by how the actual EMF affects energy or how it affects us physically.

PSYCHOMETRY:

a). Was an item brought to the location that holds an imprint of something, or someone, from the past where there may exist an energy or Spirit connection that has attached itself to the item?

b). Was the building constructed out of materials from a location that held a great deal of residual energy or emotion? An example of this would be using scrap metal or material from a ship or structure that had been the scene of a traumatic event where perhaps people died or were injured and the emotions and energy could have become imbedded in the recycled material.

THE PEOPLE THEMSELVES:

a). The high energy and hormone changes that occur in adolescents and teenagers has been linked to several occurrences of poltergeist activity.

b). Conducting séances or using Ouija Boards has been thought to open portals or vortexes through which ghosts can pass.

c). Occasional visits from loved ones when there seems to be a sadness or a needing moment or thought from those still in the physical. This longing may draw in a visit from a dearly departed loved one. These visiting apparitions are not tormented, trapped souls that are tied as ghosts to the physical dimension because of some traumatic, emotional, or materialistic reason, but rather a visiting spirit that may just come in for the moment to comfort the loved ones still here in physical life at a time of great need. People have also often spoken of bedside apparitions of loved ones who appear shortly after their crossing and of guardians and relatives who have visited them, seeming to watch over and greet them, and then slowly fade away. Oftentimes, skeptics will say it is our imagination that creates this image to comfort us while we are in the depths of our grief, but when more then one person describes the same thing without having ever told the other one beforehand, it is hard to explain away as imagination.

d). We do have to mention that there are psychological disorders that can also contribute to reports of being haunted. In such instances, discretion must be advised.

There may be many other reasons, but these can give us a clue as to why modern locations can, although less frequent then older historical sites, also experience paranormal phenomena.

Most of the places we investigate when we delve into the realms of the paranormal, however, are much older historical places. In these places where there has been long-term human occupancy and especially those where, additionally, there has been extreme emotion, something traumatic having occurred or a physical or materialistic connection to something, evidence of a haunting seems to be prevalent.

Some good places we have found to investigate are buildings like:

- Old factories or mills
- Old Universities
- Schoolhouses
- Barns
- No longer used sanatoriums

- Hospitals
- Prisons
- Battlefields
- Taverns
- Restaurants

Private Homes

These places can hold many imprints of residual energy as well as interactive energy that can be captured as evidence when recording for EVP. Older homes and private residences are also great places to investigate for signs of a haunting. Most of these were originally businesses, such as taverns, bed and breakfasts, or even brothels in times long ago. So many people once passed through their doors over history. Much of this energy may stay behind in the halls, walls, and furnishings of the structure. It is important to always ask, in advance, for permission to investigate these historical places. Be respectful and aware of safety.

Cemeteries

Many cemeteries have both modern and more ancient burial sites and investigating a cemetery can be an excellent way to start out as a paranormal investigator. Since we theorize that ghosts are not too particular about time and space, we recommended being safe and respectful and going during the times when it is light outside. (Additionally, most cemeteries are closed to the public at dusk.)

All of these places and more can yield some phenomenal paranormal evidence and abound with history. It is a good idea to do a little historical research before you go to a place to investigate. It may give you many clues as to what may have happened there and why it would be conducive to being a haunted location. History has a fascination for me and in my writings I always attempt to intertwine the historical reality of the location with any paranormal evidence we discover. It's educational, as well as enlightening.

Someday we ourselves may be part of the historical research and pursuits of future paranormal investigators.

I hope these thoughts were helpful should you decide to venture out into the world of paranormal research.

21.

A Look at Cryptozoology

There are other "Spooky and Creepy" aspects of the paranormal besides ghosts and many are within fields of study about things not totally proven. Such a paranormal subject is Cryptozoology.

Cryptozoology is the study of "animals" whose existence is subjective. It is based on legends and accounts by people who have claimed to have seen strange creatures. It is also a composite of literary legends telling of mythical creatures with unusual and even magical powers, such as a Unicorn. Some of these creatures have been the subject of stories throughout hundreds, even thousands, of years or more. It is this fascination that lures cryptozoologists to venture out for solid proof that creatures, such as Bigfoot, The Loch Ness monster, The Abominable Snowman or Yeti, Mothman, Chupacabra, and many others actually exist.

Scientists do not consider Cryptozoology to be a real field of scientific research because the evidence of the existence of these strange creatures is circumstantial and not based on actual facts. But throughout time, people with no connections to each other have claimed to have seen and described the same thing when referring to some of these creatures. It is very similar to our ghost studies. So many people have had encounters with apparitions and even captured these anomalies on film, but we can still not solidly prove the existence of ghosts. But along with ghosts, "Cryptids" (as they are referred to) encounters are very real to those who have experienced them. I can most assuredly tell you about encounters I have had that will remain imprinted in my mind for the rest of my life. I have no doubt that what I saw or experienced was very real. Plus the fact that so many others have corroborated similar encounters gives credence to the existence of these mysterious entities and creatures. I guess the same way UFO sightings and Alien encounters are shrouded in suspicion, so too are cryptids and ghosts.

Let's talk a bit about some of the more famous cryptids that Crytozoologists have studied. There is the Sasquatch or Big Foot. This creature supposedly hides out in the forests and mountains and is very large and covered with hair. It is said to have a very pungent odor and high-pitched wail. Numerous videos and photos, as well as footprint casts have come forth claiming to be of this creature. Its counterpart in the cold climate and high mountains of Tibet is the Yeti or Abominable Snowman. Then there is the spooky red-eyed, half man–half bird Mothman, whose presence is said to be a death omen and another bat-winged creature with the head of a horse and tale of a snake called the Jersey Devil. Water creatures like Loch Ness Monster of Scotland and Champ of Lake Champlain are huge serpent-like creatures thought to resemble dinosaurs that have long since become extinct. Some cryptids like the Chupacabra and Jackalope walk on four legs and resemble several different species of animals blended into one but with scary overtones.

There are so many variations in the creatures that encompass cryptozoology. It's not just about the most current and well known that researchers are looking for, like Bigfoot, but also ancient and even biblical entities. Cryptozoology could encompass Angels and demons, mermaids, vampires, werewolves, ghosts, unicorns, Cyclops, centaurs, fairies, elves, leprechauns, giant sea creatures, dragons, gargoyles, aliens, and on and on. Here is a good website to show you just how extensive the list can be http://www.newanimal.org/. It is interesting though that some of the creatures that originally were considered cryptids were discovered to be real. An example of this is the Giant squid which for so many years was the subject of many a novel about ships and sailors' encounters with the creature. When one of these monsters was actually found and now lays on display in a maritime museum, the creature is no longer a cryptid and therefore no longer part of Cryptozoology, but now becomes part of Zoology.

So, the possibilities are still out there for some of these strange and mysterious creatures. Perhaps this is why the subject is so inviting and so many researchers are still in search of these things. It's a quest, just like our ghostly investigations, to prove that something else besides what is known exists. It's the gray area and the actual proof positive for the existence of these creatures that fascinates us. One of the best characteristics of the human mind is our imagination. Cryptozoology is the perfect subject to stimulate our fantastical side. Its subject matter is interesting to explore and enjoy.

22.

The Paranormal Investigators Toolbox

Author Note

I can't specifically give brand names that will be the best for each individual investigator or team, but those mentioned here have worked well for me and my group. I am sure that other brands would do equally well. Always research your equipment as you would your ghosts.

Doing research in the paranormal doesn't have to be expensive. There are some basic tools that are helpful that you can obtain to begin. If you really decide this is a passion for you, then there are more devices that you can add along the way.

I recommend starting off with an open mind and interest in the paranormal.

Cassette and micro-cassette recorders will capture EVP.

I captured my very first and longest EVP back in April of 2001 using a cassette recorder, but I highly recommend using digital recorders.

Smaller, no moving parts, and ease of use in recording and playback are just a few good reasons to use digital recorders during investigations.

There are several name brands of digital recorders. We have found the noisier the circuitry within the recorder, the more energy the spirits have to work with and the greater the chance of capturing EVP messages. Some of the recorders noted for getting good EVP are the RR-DR60, QR100, and the RR-QR80 by Panasonic. Because they are hard to find and no longer manufactured by Panasonic, they are rather expensive. But other recorders, such as Sony and Olympus models like the Sony ICD-B7 and B17 (same recorder but with voice activation) are very conducive to capturing EVP. Voice activation is always a good feature to look for on a recorder because it reduces the amount of time spent on analysis after an investigation. We find that EVP messages are generally short in duration. We theorize this is because it takes a great deal of energy on the part of a ghost to manifest a message through the noise in the recorder.

Digital photo and video cameras are also an essential part of an investigation.

Both 35mm and disposable cameras have become less desirable than digital still cameras that allow us to take unlimited pictures with no additional costs. This is not to say that the older methods of paranormal photography did not capture phenomenal images. Some of the classic ghost photographs were captured on these types of cameras. But most investigators today use digital and video cameras, many of which have the added feature of having night shot and also infrared capabilities. These features are a bonus and a great asset to the paranormal investigator.

Some of the best evidence presented has been in the way of infrared photography. Leo Monfet has captured some amazing images on infrared at haunted locations. (Several can be seen on our website at www.ectoweb. com at this link http://ectoweb.com/Investigations/Tortilla%20Flat/Tortilla%20Flat.htm#Tortilla_Flat_Restaurant).

If money is no object for you and your team, there are expensive infrared and thermal imaging cameras available. The thermal imaging cameras can pick up heat and cool signatures in their view. They are more portable with the advancement of technology, but are still quite expensive.

EMF meters are a very important part of any paranormal investigators equipment portfolio.

Whenever there is a spike in the amount of EMF (not attributed to natural occurrences, such as electrical wiring or equipment nearby), there seems to be a prevalence of paranormal activity. Some well-known name brands are the ELF detector, Trifield meter, and the K2 meter. You can also use something as simple as a compass.

These three pieces of equipment—camera, recorder, and EMF meter—are, in my opinion, your key items to take along on an investigation. They are all within most of our affordable budget range.

Here are a few other tools that paranormal investigators find useful. Many researchers like to carry along:

Temperature sensors.

Paranormal investigators watch for fluctuations in temperature readings as a key sign that there may be ghostly energy present. A sudden drop in temperature readings is a key sign that there may be something paranormal happening causing the heat energy to be drained from the area. Use of this energy can help a paranormal manifestation. Most investigators use digital temperature sensors but there are also more expensive and sophisticated temperature readers that operate with lasers that shoot out a beam to read the surrounding temperature.

Radio Hack box.

One of the newest pieces of equipment groups have begun using is a radio type device, which continuously scans in between stations and sometimes produces messages within the static significant to the investigation. The "Hack box," a modified radio, is one example of this type of equipment. There are other devices that use syllables and phonemes, such as the Ovilus, which form messages from within the vocabulary of their database. These messages sometimes sound very robotic, but can be readily deciphered word forms.

New equipment seems to be popping up everyday and continues to excite and enthuse us as it pushes us closer to an understanding of this other dimension of existence; a dimension that we, after all, will be part of some day.

And then there is the common sense stuff, like a flashlight, pendulum, or dowsing rods. Don't forget water for hydration, as well as a face mask if you plan to be in an old decaying building. You may also want to bring paper and graph paper for mapping with pens and pencils. Extension cords can be handy for equipment needing it. Bring emergency numbers and contact information. Props can also be included if they would be helpful on the investigation.

I hope this helps direct you to the kind of equipment that can help you start out if you decide paranormal investigating is something you would like to try. Remember to be professional and respectful and that spirits can be just about everywhere and at anytime, day or night. You don't need to spend a lot of money to get started.

23.

A Look at Paranormal Evidence

The Explained and the Unexplained

During my twelve-plus years as a researcher and investigator into the paranormal, I have learned a great many things to look for in terms of the evidence captured. There is a great deal of what is referred to as "false-positives," in the EVP, pictures, and video that are produced following an investigation. That is why it is so important to discredit and toss out anything that can be explained as a natural occurrence or attributed to something physical.

EVP

Be mindful of how easily a physical sound can be mistaken for an EVP. In one of our investigations, one of our team members softly cleared his throat. Upon playback of one recorder we heard what sounded like a little boy saying help me in a muffled tone. When we played back the second recorder we heard the exact same sound and immediately knew this was not an EVP. Our team member then told us he had cleared his throat in a high-pitched sound while we were recording.

Equally important is the necessity of silence while you are doing an EVP session. Announce that you are recording for EVP and that it is important for other team members to be quiet and respectful during this time. No one should whisper when investigators are recording. Many a whisper has been mistaken for an EVP since we often do capture legitimate EVP that sound like whispers.

Another thing to always watch out for when recording for EVP is rubbing against the recorder. You can easily rub your fingers on the surface of the recorder when you are going to shut it off after closing an EVP session. You could also rub the recorder against your clothing. Additionally, you could place your recorder on a surface and slide it against this surface and produce sounds that are not EVP. Mike and I have tested this several times and often a rubbing or scratching sound can appear to be a voice or EVP when, in actuality, it is a naturally occurring sound that can be easily explained as a normal occurrence.

One last thing I would like to mention regarding EVP. We use editing software when we are analyzing our EVP. We transfer our recordings from the recorder into these audio programs. But one thing that should remain very important to the serious EVP researcher is not to overuse editing on an EVP and make it into something it is not. In the beginning, Mike and I tried to analyze every EVP recording we captured; even those that were not clear at all. This would take hours of time and effort. Over the years, we have come to realize that the Spirits are able to bring through clearer messages. These messages require very little editing other then perhaps amplitude. With this said, Mike and I focus on the clearer messages that we receive. This is the evidence you want to bring forth to offer up as solid proof for the phenomena of EVP.

Orbs

I will speak now on paranormal photography and videography. Everyone knows the phenomena of the so-called "orb." What is an orb? Oftentimes, in photos we see a white or colored glowing balls or many of them in our pictures. Over the years, we have come to understand that there are many explanations for these extras in paranormal photography and videos. Here are some of the reasons these can appear that are not paranormal in nature at all:

- Often times dust and moisture exist in places we investigate. Dust exists everywhere and when people are walking through a location they stir these dust particles up and they are floating all about while investigators are snapping away taking pictures. This is simply dust and not a ghost!

- Or, we could be outside investigating a cemetery and it may have rained or is misting and our photos will capture moisture orbs. Videos can produce these same natural occurring extras in their clips as well.

However, there seem to be anomalies of an orb-like nature that cannot be explained away by the sources previously mentioned. Sometimes there seems to be a moving opaque-like anomaly that occurs in one shot and then is gone in the next which was taken within a second or two later. This may be something paranormal and can be further corroborated if accompanied during the investigation by a medium or psychic who feels a ghostly presence at this exact time.

Also "orbs" that seem to respond to investigators may indicate a non-physical presence. We have had cases where we sense children or animal spirits and an orb that is lower to the ground has appeared. Another occurred when our medium told us there was a spirit sitting in the chair in the room we were investigating, and in one of the pictures taken at this exact time, a milky-white orb, that seemed to be moving, was seen on the seat of the chair.

Moving Insect. *Photo courtesy of Mike Sullivan*

Insects

Insects can also create false evidence in investigations. Oftentimes, a bug will fly by when a picture is being taken and it appears as a glowing object in the photo. This is not paranormal. We have several examples of this.

Mist

Mist and smoke can also seem to produce eerie images that look very ghostly, but these, too, could be natural occurrences and explained as normal. For example, if someone is smoking or if the air is cold, a "mist" might seem to appear on a photograph when it is really someone's breath or the smoke from a cigarette.

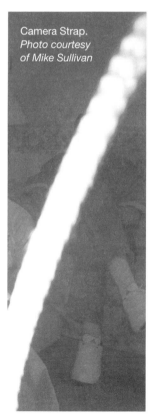

Camera Strap.
Photo courtesy of Mike Sullivan

Items on Your Person

If a piece of your hair or a camera strap gets in the line of your lens while you are taking a picture, it can appear as an anomaly in the photograph. This must be discredited.

Car Lights

If you are filming a video and shooting at a window as a car passes by, this can create what appears to be a floating apparition. It is not.

There are many naturally occurring things that can easily be misinterpreted as being paranormal evidence. The seasoned investigator must be well trained for this non-paranormal evidence. That is why it is very important for all the investigators to have their input, so that the evidence is completely analyzed and non-biased. What you are then left with, after debunking that which is not paranormal, is that which is most likely the real deal and validated evidence in both EVP and photography.

I am sure there is even more evidence that I have not mentioned here that is often proven not to be paranormal. This section will simply give you a better idea of some of the evidence that needs to be strongly analyzed and oftentimes discredited before researchers present it to the public. It makes us all look that much more credible and professional to bring forth the evidence we are then left with that remains unexplained and truly paranormal.

Good luck out there.

Personal Paranormal Encounters

24.

A Ghost Story
Columbia, South America

Author Note

Sometimes, an interest in investigating ghosts begins with experiences outside one's own back door in some far off location, which is the case in the following story. Then the love of the hunt follows them throughout life—and into New England!

There are many traditions and beliefs regarding ghosts and the Afterlife in South American countries. Most of the folks from there are firm believers in the Afterlife and have a high respect for the dead. Many also believe and even practice Santeria, which is a form of magic. So I thought I would share a short story that was related to me by a friend and co-worker from Columbia. It is an amazing accounting of a true event.

Culture and tradition are rich in South America. Both the Aztecs and the Incas practiced different forms of worship and held spirits, witches, demons, and souls in high regards and firmly believed that when dealing with these, you must invoke protection or ritual practices to prevent them from causing harm. Each tribe had its witch doctor and the many archaeological digs have discovered many talismans and symbols that were used by these people to honor and show respect for the inhabitants of the Afterlife and protect them against those they considered dark forces. Many of the cultures were polytheistic and worshipped many different Gods, and objects, some of which were the sun, moon, stars, animals, and idols.

Much of the nation is now monotheistic and Catholicism is the main religion, but the roots of centuries long past and their practices run deep and many people are firm believers in the Spirit world. Such is this story about a troubled ghost.

My friend's family owned a farm in Columbia. It was a nice house, but everyone who lived there was always scared to stay because each one had, on more then one occasion, seen the ghost of a woman in one had, on more then one occasion, seen the ghost of a woman in black. Everyone would always corroborate the same story. They would see her float through the kitchen, never saying a word or looking their way and then she would pass through the wall. It was always the same pattern every time they saw her.

Those who stayed longer then others became used to seeing her, but never comfortable with it, and sooner or later, each one of them could no longer stay at the farm. The people who would come in to clean also experienced the seemingly unaware ghostly woman's apparition. It was as if she was searching for something and needed to repeat this action over and over without resolve.

This type of haunting, as I've mentioned earlier, is called a residual haunting. The ghost is not aware of the presence of people and does not interact with anyone. In many cases, paranormal researchers believe these spirits are doomed to repeat this pattern forever with no hope of dissipating the routine. This is, however, not what happened in this residual haunting case.

After losing so many tenants to the farm and not being able to financially maintain it, my friend's cousin decided that he would go and take up residence there and seek to understand what this entity was looking for and the history that might be behind this repetitive action. He wondered who she might be. Had she lived there at one time? The farm was very old so it is likely that many people had lived within its walls at one time or another. Long-term human occupancy is one of the main factors in a haunting. So the young man went to live on the farm. Almost immediately he experienced the woman in a long, black dress passing through the kitchen and out through the wall towards the outer part of the house. He admitted to being quite startled, but not really frightened. He described her as almost solid and so clear as she manifested and then quickly disappearing. He called out to her but there was no response.

"Who are you and what is your name?" he called.

There was never an answer, just the same repeating action each time it occurred. How could the young man help her if he never got a response? So, one day, he decided to follow her exact path and then draw, in his mind, a line to the outside that she would have proceeded to. He went outside just in front of the kitchen and noticed a small bump to the otherwise level ground. He took a shovel and began digging in the area. After a while he hit something solid. As he continued digging he unearthed tiny little bones that appeared to be human baby bones. He called the local authorities who later identified the bones as that of an infant child buried there long ago.

The young man and the authorities researched old historical records and found many families who had lived on the farm and had several children. Although it is not clear as to the identity of the child, the records did indicate that a young child had died there. Since it was nearly impossible to trace this little child to any living relatives, the young man decided that the respectful thing to do was to take the bones and give this child a proper burial, and that he did.

Over the next days and weeks, there was no sign of the woman in a black dress appearing and disappearing on her regular routine. He stayed over a month expecting to once again see her, but there was never again a sighting. He believes this woman was doomed to repeat following the path to her baby's bones until the child was found and properly laid to rest. Having found the child brought resolution to her continued wandering and she could now rest in peace. The farm was never again haunted by the woman in black and people could once again live in the home undisturbed.

Sometimes these wandering souls are just seeking a long-passed event to be resolved for them. The energy of this emotional event causes them to continue to wander until a discovery is made. That is what I believe happened here in this haunting story and provides a testament to the fact that with a little interest and attention to the reason behind a residual haunting there can be help and justice for a troubled soul.

27.
Blair

Story by Jessica Mackey

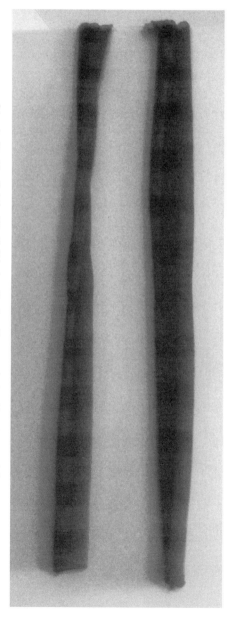

The scarf that appeared in the dream.
Photo courtesy of Karen Mossey

My wonderful and forever friend, Blair, died June 16, 2001, from injuries sustained in a car accident. Since that time, I have often sensed her with me. She seems to watch over me and appears to me often during stressful and painful times in my life. I know she is one of my guardians. Many of my journal entries are encounters with Blair. Following are a few recent and very remarkable contacts by her.

She first appeared to me in a dream where she was at my friend Jen's mother's house. It was a frightening dream and I don't understand it completely. She showed herself hanging on the porch with my sweater scarf around her neck. It was awful. I asked her to myself: *Why show me this horrible image of you hanging there Blair?* It remained imprinted in my mind for such a long time. All I could think of

The magazine that came in the mail.
Photo courtesy of Jessica Mackey

a long time. All I could think of was that she was signaling an end to something. Maybe it was an end to my married life. The dream happened on October 3rd. That was the day that my ex-husband had left me in 2010 and only 10 days before what would have been my wedding anniversary.

The second night she came again. In this ghostly dream she kept showing me the number 1703. It was everywhere! It would appear in the steam of the mirror when I showered. I would see it written in many places. In this dream I was married to a wonderful man. Perhaps she was telling me that he would live at an address with the number 1703. The connection was not entirely clear. The number, however, certainly was.

Now I switch from dreams to reality. This is where things start to happen during waking state. It was the very next day after the "1703" dream and I had come home from work and picked up my mail from the mailbox. I brought it in and laid in down on the counter. When I moved some of it aside, there in front of me was a magazine entitled *BLAIR*! I had never ordered this magazine and never even seen or heard of this company before in my entire life. When I saw it, I totally freaked out and screamed. This was real now! I threw it across the kitchen floor. My son, Connor, looked at me and said, "What the heck is wrong with you Mom?" I immediately took a picture of it.

The next day I was at my friend Kristen's hair salon and she handed me a check — and I couldn't believe what I was seeing. The check number was "1703." I had just been talking to Kristen about everything that had happened with the magazine. I know this was Blair's way of telling us she was there and listening to everything we had just said.

The dreams continued. I would awake at the same time every night and she would be standing in my doorway looking at me. She would not speak and would never cross the threshold to come into my room. She would just stand there and stare at me from the entrance. I would sense her presence constantly. She was always there. But what was she trying to communicate to me? Was she just there to protect me or watch over me? I was never scared when I saw her, but felt very anxious and confused. I could not figure out exactly what she was trying to tell me. I journaled every occurrence.

The final dream involved a three-car accident that happened around Danny and Kim's store. That was my old stomping ground.

For some reason, I had to get to the store on Dracut Road because the accidents were bad. One woman was killed and my ex husband was walking around like a zombie. I don't know what this all meant, but I know that Blair told me it was important to get to the store.

I still don't fully understand the meaning of all of the communications I have received from Blair, but I know that she has a real reason to be here for me. I sense her presence around me so often. She is a strong and persistent guardian and relentless when attempting to get her messages through. She knows that I do acknowledge her. I never received that magazine *Blair* again, so I know that the dreams and visits during that time were especially important for her and that she worked very hard to influence the physical world and bring that magazine and message forward to me. It was a very strong validation of her presence in my life.

I am still not sure what 1703 means or why she cannot cross the threshold of the doorway into my bedroom. I also don't totally understand why she showed herself hanging with my scarf. It seems she is strong with me during difficult times in my life and knows my thoughts and needs. Perhaps she was trying to scare some sense into me and make me realize that the things happening were for the best.

We don't always understand everything the spirit world is trying to tell us or how they mysteriously work in our lives, but knowing that they do is acknowledgment enough for them and a validation for us. They are okay knowing that we get it and are trying to understand. She will keep at it until eventually I will figure it all out. Thank you Blair. I love and miss you so much!

26.
The Coin

The coin. *Photo courtesy of Cathy O'Dea*

Not a day goes by that I don't miss my loved ones who have passed on. I think of my son, Rob, everyday. I miss my mother and father so much too, but they lived out long lives. Some days are worse then others for me. Birthdays and the dates of their passing are especially hard. It has been twelve years since Rob made his transition and ten for my father now, but the sadness of missing them , though it has softened over the years, never goes away. I still have, what I it has softened over the years, never goes away. I still have, what I refer to as, "Bad Rob days," where the hurt and sadness is harder then other days. Such was one day several years ago.

I was having a really hard time at work because I became overwhelmed with sadness from missing my son, Rob. I can't remember what exactly had triggered it. Perhaps it was something or someone that reminded me of him and I just couldn't get out of the depression. Taking a nice walk or jog always seems to help me and settle my anxiety. It is something I would do often at lunchtime during work. Today was a definite for a jog. I just had to get away for awhile.

It was a nice day and I figured as soon as I got outside, I could break down and cry and let it all out. That is just what happened. I talked out loud to Rob and my dad (my mother had not passed away at this time).

I said, "Rob, Dad, I am sorry that I am crying so hard. I know that it makes you sad to see me cry like this, but I can't help myself because I just miss you so much."

Just seconds after I had spoken these very words, a car drove by me. I looked at the license plate and was so shocked but at the same time soothed. The license plate said "MISS U." My heart was filled with such joy. I knew, without a doubt, they were with me and answering me.

I continued on my jog down to the Fish and Game and back around in a completely different state of mind then what I had started in. There was a simple smile upon my face. My heart felt so much lighter and I sensed a spiritual presence around me. As I turned the corner and headed back to work, I saw something shining on the ground ahead. I stopped and bent down to see it. There on the ground was a beautiful gold coin. I picked it up and brushed it off. There were no words on it but simply an angel standing on clouds on both sides of the coin. This was assuredly a sign from Rob and my dad. I picked it up and put it in my pocket and gazed up to the sky with a huge smile and said, "Thank you, Rob. Thank you, Dad." They had given me all I needed to let me know they are still with me and always will be.

Several years later, I experienced another such day. I was at the town dump emptying trash. My good friend, Kevin, who was also a great friend to my son, Rob, called me. I had been having a very blue "Bad Rob Day." Kevin and I started reminiscing about the many awesome things Rob did and how funny he was. I couldn't stop crying. I should be happy when I think of these fond memories, but it was, once again, the overwhelming sadness of missing him. I was holding the phone in one hand talking to Kevin and started emptying the trash into the bin with the other. As I got to the bottom of the barrel, there stuck on the bottom was the exact same type of golden angel coin that had come to me several years previous while on my jog. I couldn't believe my eyes! Had I not looked down, it would have toppled into the trash bin. I had no idea how it could have gotten there, other then having been sent, once again, from my son, Rob. There it was once more on the same type of sad day that I had had several years before. I cleaned it off and told Kevin. He was amazed and told me to send him a picture of it. I now take this as Rob's and my dad's sign and their way to let me know that I don't have to worry about them. They want me to know that they are fine and always there for me. Their wish for me is to live my life in a happier way.

I now have two of these angel coins and every time I feel the sadness coming on I pick them up and hold them and look up and say "Love you, Rob. Love you, Dad."

27.
Precious Stone

Story by Sandy Stone

Precious Stone, the kitty. *Photo courtesy of Sandy Stone*

On January 9, 2012, I made a decision I have always hoped I would never have to make in life. My dearest cat, Precious Stone, was suffering from an incurable brain tumor that had changed her behavior drastically; I needed to put her to sleep. She went from a very loving cat to attacking me when I was leaving the house to go to work. She hissed at me instead of wanting a kiss or giving me kitty kisses, as she usually did when I came home from work. I became afraid of her because of her mood swings.

My Precious Stone would have been 12 years old this year.

Precious was a very special cat. She helped me get over my mother's death in 2000. My cat and I were the same zodiac sign of Libra. September 24th we would celebrate our birthdays together with a cake. I even put candles on it. We would (rather I would) then blow them out. (No, I never gave her a piece of cake.) She always knew what to do to make me feel better. Her love was so sincere and I loved her deeper than any cat I have ever had. She was my soul mate cat. We had an incredible bond. I've had never had a relationship like this with any of my other cats. Precious always understood me and I understood her.

Since her passing, I have had so many spiritual and phenomenal experiences that let me know her spirit is still with me. The very night after having to put her to sleep, I saw a shadow move in front of the couch. Over the next two days, and always at night, I started seeing Precious walking through the bedrooms and then into my bedroom. There was this movement I could see even in the darkness. I could see it out of the corner of my eye. When I'd turned to look, it was gone. It lasted only a few seconds. I thought I was hallucinating at first, due to my severe grief over losing her. I wanted so much for it to be real, but I thought it was just my imagination. So I ignored it.

On Friday afternoon, the 13th of January, as I was stepping out of the shower, I clearly saw a set of white paws walking into my bedroom. I stood frozen and just watched. I was shocked when I saw her white chest. Then, as quickly as I had seen her, she disappeared. This time it was not night. There was no darkness. The light was good for me to see her. This is always what she would have done. She would be there waiting for me when I came out of the shower. Now I knew I wasn't just imaging it. It was real!

On Saturday morning at 3:10 a.m., I heard her footsteps coming into my bedroom, just as I would have heard them time and time again when she was alive and always right before she would jump onto my bed to let me know she was hungry. But when I opened my eyes, there was nothing there.

Then Sunday morning at 4:10 a.m., I heard her *meow* twice. This is how she would let me know that she wanted me to feed her. That night, I caught a glimpse of something moving quickly across the kitchen. Suddenly, I saw Precious walking to her feeding area. Within seconds she was gone.

When I went to my bedroom, I noticed her glowing eyes under my bed looking at me. She was crouched down. In a flash, she was gone. That was all I saw of her that week. Perhaps she had given me all the signs I needed to let me know that her spirit would remain with me to give me a measure of comfort through my grief.

A week has passed by and it was Saturday morning. I couldn't believe what I was seeing. There, in plain sight, was her favorite toy. I was surprised because I should have noticed it before. What's interesting about this, is that it was her blue toy. I feel inside that she sent the blue toy as a message to let me know that she was sad and had the blues and is missing me, too. Precious wanted me to know that she was still spiritually with me and always would be.

I don't think I've heard or seen the last of Precious Stone. She will find a way to keep in touch with me from the Otherside.

I have never had an experience like this before and I've had several cats in my lifetime. The difference is, I have never had such a strong emotional and spiritual bond with a cat. Even when I was sick, she would take care of me. If I had chills, she would warm me up. I called her "Nurse Precious." One day when she was a kitten, I came home sick and ran through the house to vomit in the bathroom. She was watching me. After feeding her, I went right to bed. I noticed she kept jumping onto my bed to check on me. She would be playing with her toys and then she would come on my bed. When I would turn to look at her, she had her front paws on my back and she would stare at me as if she was taking my vital signs.

Then she would go back to playing with her toys on the floor. She did this several times. It always amazed me.

When I first met my Precious Stone as a little kitty, she came to me with so much love. It was as if she already knew me. We had just met and already she was giving me a whole bunch of kitty kisses.

She seemed to know that it was her home. There was an instant sense of comfort and welcome in my home and with me. I had never experienced anything like that with any of my previous cats. I felt as though she was my Angel Cat that was assigned to me from God to help me during my mother's illness, her passing, and afterwards. Now I feel her assignment is over and she has been called back. But I am sure she will keep in touch and I will see her again.

I will forever love you, Precious!

Resources

www.coltsfoot.net/maine/two/howard1.html

www.csni.org/LaconiaStateSchool/Laconia%20State%20 Cemetery.doc

www.csni.org/LaconiaStateSchool/laconia%20Sun%20 Article040407.pdf

www.csni.org/LaconiaStateSchool/Timeline4.4.07.pdf

www.hampton.lib.nh.us/hampton/history/dow/chap10/ dow10_23.htm

www.hudsonctv.com/Cablecast/Public/Main. aspx?ChannelID=1

www.seacoastnh.com/Famous_People/Framers_of_Freedom/ Mary_Bartlett/

www3.gendisasters.com/massachusetts/17002/salisbury- beach-ma-schooner-florida-wrecked-feb1896

Index of Places

About the Author

Karen Mossey is the author of *Spooky Creepy New England* and *Spooky Creepy New England 2*. She resides in Merrimack, New Hampshire, and enjoys traveling throughout the New England area and beyond to investigate cases of paranormal activity. Investigating haunted places for over twelve years, she has journeyed throughout the United States, from New England all the way to San Francisco, where she and her team were able to sleep overnight in the very haunted and infamous penitentiary of Alcatraz. She has also lived in Germany for eleven years and has traveled extensively throughout Europe.

Karen and her team have captured phenomenal ghostly EVP (Electronic Voice Phenomena), photographs, and videos that are unsurpassed in the paranormal community. You can hear and see this amazing supernatural evidence on their website www.ectoweb. com. Karen writes a monthly article about these encounters and related paranormal subjects for the *State Line Review* newspaper. She has been a member of the A-Trans-C (American Association of Trans-Communication) since 2001, and has been on the *Maury Povitch* television show and many radio and television programs. Her EVPs have been featured in the trailer for the Movie *White Noise*, starring Michael Keaton, and an episode of *Ghost Whisperer*, with Jennifer Love Hewitt. Many of Karen's EVP messages are world renown, like the "I Love You" EVP she received in 2003 from her father who had passed on in 2002.

She has four children and three grandchildren. Her daughter, grandson, and granddaughter love joining her on many of her paranormal investigations. They have nicknamed themselves "3G Paranormal," standing for three generations of paranormal investigators. Karen has a passion for history and believes history and paranormal activity are intertwined. In her spare time, she enjoys having fun with her family, reading, writing, and watching scary movies and shows. She also enjoys foreign films and especially spooky movies from South Korea.